LASER FOCUS

HOW TO FOCUS ON WHAT MATTERS MOST

Grant Pierce

Copyright © 2024 **Grant Pierce**

All rights reserved. No part of this book may be reproduced or transmitted in any form or by any means, electronic or mechanical, including photocopying, recording, or by any information storage and retrieval system, without permission in writing from the publisher.

Introduction

In a world where distractions lurk around every corner, demanding our attention with dogged persistence, the ability to retain concentration has become a treasured asset. This rare skill offers clarity, productivity, and inner calm despite the turmoil. However, in our efforts to concentrate, we find that we are caught in a paradoxical conundrum: the more we desire to be the sole recipient of our undivided attention, the more difficult it appears to be to achieve.

Just for a moment, picture yourself sitting down at your desk, intent on doing work that is of critical importance. Your phone is buzzing with notifications, your inbox is flooded with emails, and your mind is wandering to discussions that are still incomplete and deadlines that are drawing near. You put up an effort to concentrate, yet your concentration is as easily lost as sand through your fingers, leaving you feeling disappointed and unsatisfied. Does this sound familiar to you?

This is the crux of the attention challenge, which is a conflict between our desire for profound engagement and the constant pull of distractions. The terrain of attention has gone through a transformation as a result of our modern era, which is characterized by rapid connectedness and information overload. We are assaulted with stimuli, from social media updates to breaking news alerts, creating a fight for our attention.

The question is why is it so important to focus? Beyond simple productivity, attention is the road to mastery. It is the key that unlocks creative potential, the ability to solve problems, and the capabilities to do significant things. Whether you're a student attempting to thrive in academics, an entrepreneur navigating a competitive marketplace, or simply an individual seeking joy in daily life, your capacity to concentrate intensely directly influences your performance and well-being.

On the other hand, the road to prolonged attention is difficult and riddled with obstacles. Our brains, genetically built to seek novelty and react to stimuli, today contend with a plethora of distractions that erode our cognitive stamina. The appeal of multitasking is that it offers efficiency but leads to divided attention and lower performance. The continual ping of alerts hijacks our focus, leaving us in a perpetual state of split attention.

Amidst this cacophony of distractions, recovering our concentration becomes a fundamental exercise of self-mastery—a path of knowing our mind's weaknesses and acquiring the discipline to navigate our attentional terrain purposefully in this book, **"LASER FOCUS"** we start with a study of the attention challenge. We will dig into the science of attention, deconstruct the misconceptions around multitasking, and find the tactics for deep, sustained focus in an era of distractions. But more than that, we will reveal the deep influence of attention on our relationships, well-being, and personal fulfillment.

Throughout these pages, you will discover practical ideas, useful practices, and thought-provoking thoughts to help you on your focus journey. Whether you want to recover control over your attention, better your professional performance, or cultivate deeper relationships in your personal life, this book is your companion in mastering the discipline of uninterrupted focus.

So, let us go together on this transforming quest—to regain our concentration, uncover our potential, and appreciate the richness of life that emerges when we learn to fully pay attention.

What to Expect

Welcome to "Cultivating Focus in a Distracted World"! In this book, we embark on a transformative journey to explore the complexities of attention and distraction management. Here's what you can expect from this exploration:

Understanding the Dynamics of Attention

Gain insights into the nature of attention, from external distractions like digital overload to internal challenges such as cognitive biases and emotional fluctuations. Learn how these factors impact focus and productivity in various aspects of life.

Evidence-Based Strategies and Techniques

Discover a comprehensive toolkit of evidence-based strategies and practical techniques for cultivating attentional focus amidst distractions. Explore mindfulness practices, productivity methods, cognitive tools, and boundary-setting strategies to optimize cognitive clarity and productivity.

Real-World Applications and Case Studies

Apply the concepts and techniques discussed in real-world scenarios through practical examples and case studies. Explore how individuals in different contexts leverage focus-enhancing strategies to achieve goals, overcome challenges, and thrive in today's fast-paced world.

Personal Growth and Resilience

Embark on a journey of personal growth and resilience as you develop adaptive thinking, problem-solving skills, and emotional regulation. Learn to navigate distractions with intention, cultivate deep engagement with tasks, and reclaim your cognitive clarity.

Actionable Steps and Implementation Plan

Walk away with a personalized action plan for managing distractions and enhancing focus in your daily life. Develop consistency in practice and commit to continuous improvement in attentional skills.

Reflection and Integration

Reflect on your progress and insights gained throughout the book. Integrate focus-enhancing techniques into your routines and embrace a lifestyle of mindfulness, productivity, and purpose.

Empowerment and Transformation

Experience the transformative power of cultivating focus amidst a distracted world. Feel empowered to reclaim your attention, amplify your productivity, and lead a more intentional and fulfilling life.

Introduction 3

Chapter 1: The Evolution of Attention............................ 11

    The Dawn of Human Attention 11

    The Impact of Industrialization on Attention ... 12

    Adapting to a Distracting World....................... 13

    Understanding Modern Distractions................. 14

    The Temptation of Multitasking....................... 14

    The Dilemma of Information Overload............ 15

Chapter 2: The Science of Attention................................ 18

    The Neurobiology of Attention 18

    The Mastery of Attention..................................21

    Brain Mechanics and Focus..............................22

    Practical Implications for Enhancing Focus.....25

    The Dynamic Brain...30

Chapter 3: The Myth of Multitasking.............................. 32

    The Illusion of Multitasking 32

    The Myth of "Good" Multitaskers 34

    Practical Strategies for Task Management 35

    Redefining Productivity 36

    Mindful Technology Use 40

The Cost of Task Switching 41
Strategies for Mitigating Task-Switching Costs
.... 45
Chapter 4: The Power of Deep Work 48
Defining Deep Work 48
The Benefits of Deep Work 49
Embracing Deep Work 52
Techniques for profound focus 56
What is deep work? 57
Chapter 5: Mindfulness and Meditation 71
The Essence of Mindfulness and Meditation ... 71
Meditation Practices for Enhanced Concentration
.... 75
Zen meditation 79
Chapter 6: Building Focus Habits 84
Daily Rituals for Improved Attention 104
Chapter 7: Taming Technology 111
Strategies for Taming Technology 112
Chapter 8: Managing Distractions from Relationships ... 124
Chapter 9: Managing External Distractions 145
Strategies to Manage External Distractions 146

Chapter 10: Overcoming Internal Distractions 159

    Battling procrastination 162

    Handling Mental Blocks 169

    Strategies for Overcoming Mental Blocks 170

Chapter 11: Unleashing Brain Power 174

Chapter 12: Brain configuration and Healing during Addiction Recovery 187

Chapter 13: Battling ADHD 194

Conclusion 204

About the Author 208

Chapter 1

The Evolution of Attention

In the hectic world of the 21st century, where displays flare with limitless information and notifications demand our instant reaction, attention has become one of our most valuable resources—and simultaneously, one of our biggest difficulties to harness.

The Dawn of Human Attention

To understand our connection with attention now, we must go back through the annals of time to our earliest ancestors. Human attention, in its original form, was exquisitely attuned to the necessities of survival in the environment. Millennia ago, our primitive forefathers depended on sharp attention to hunt creatures, gather food, and dodge predators. This innate attentiveness, sculpted by natural selection, was a major role in our species' capacity to survive and multiply around the globe.

The Advent of Civilization and the Shifting Focus

As mankind migrated from nomadic tribes to sedentary civilizations, our attention experienced a remarkable development. The advent of agriculture, written language, and structured communities imposed new stimuli and demands on our cognitive skills. With the advent of ancient civilizations like Mesopotamia, Egypt, and Greece, attention became more tied to intellectual pursuits—

reading, writing, debating—laying the framework for the academic concentration that would define following epochs.

The Impact of Industrialization on Attention

The Industrial Revolution marked a key point in the history of human attention. As cultures industrialized and urbanized, the focus switched from rural activities to factory jobs and assembly lines. The repetitive nature of industrial labor needed a distinct sort of focus—disciplined and routine-driven, yet subject to boredom and tiredness. Meanwhile, the rise of print media and mass communication created new routes for attracting attention, predicting the media-saturated world of the modern age.

Enter the Digital Age: Attention in the Information Era

Fast forward to the current day, and we find ourselves in the Information Age—an era marked by remarkable technical developments and the pervasive presence of digital gadgets. Our attention is inundated from all directions: social media updates, streaming services, instant messaging, and a 24/7 news cycle. The Internet, with its immense reservoir of knowledge and pleasure, provides endless options for engagement—but at a cost.

The Paradox of Choice and Attention Scarcity

With a wealth of alternatives at our fingertips, we face the paradox of choice—a phenomenon where an excess of possibilities may overwhelm and hamper decision-making. This abundance goes beyond commercial items to information consumption, where the appeal of novelty and immediate satisfaction may splinter our attention into transient pieces. Consequently, attention has become a rare commodity in the digital era, sought by advertisers and content providers alike.

Neurological Insights: How the Brain Adapts to Distraction

Neuroscience provides light on the subtleties of human attention, demonstrating how our brains adapt—or struggle to adapt—to modern distractions. The dopamine-driven reward circuits that underpin addictive behaviors also affect our digital consumption habits, sustaining cycles of distraction and obsessive engagement. Meanwhile, our potential for sustained focus is taxed by the ongoing demands of multitasking and split attention.

Adapting to a Distracting World

In this dynamic context, managing attention is not only a question of willpower; it takes a comprehensive grasp of our cognitive constraints and adaptive methods. From mindfulness techniques to deliberate technology usage, individuals seek sanctuary from the stream of distractions, attempting to recover agency over their attentional resources.

Looking Ahead: Navigating the Future of Attention

As scientists peek into the horizon of human attention, concerns abound regarding the ramifications of our digital lifestyles on cognition and well-being. How will future technologies like augmented reality and artificial intelligence affect our relationship with attention? How can we create a healthy attitude to information intake in an era marked by continual connectivity?

In the coming chapters of this book, we will go deeper into these concerns, examining practical approaches and ideas for mastering attention in the age of distraction. Our quest begins with studying the foundations of our attentional development and continues towards developing new routes for cognitive resilience and uninterrupted attention.

Understanding Modern Distractions

In the maze of modern life, distractions lurk around every corner, clamoring for our attention and fragmenting our focus. To traverse this complicated world efficiently, we must first grasp the nature of these distractions—what they are, how they emerge, and why they offer a challenge to our cognitive well-being.

The Pervasiveness of Digital Distractions

At the core of contemporary diversions is the digital sphere, a huge ecosystem of knowledge and entertainment accessible at our fingertips. Social media platforms call with endless scrolling of handpicked material, alerts ding ceaselessly, and addicting Smartphone applications seduce us with quick satisfaction. Our electronics, once aids of productivity, have evolved into portals of continual distraction, blurring the lines between work and leisure.

The Temptation of Multitasking

In the quest for efficiency, many fall to the attraction of multitasking—a myth maintained by the assumption that juggling many things concurrently leads to better productivity. However, research demonstrates a plain reality: multitasking degrades performance, reduces attention, and adds to cognitive overload. The human brain, developed for depth of attention, falters when assaulted with concurrent information.

The Dilemma of Information Overload

In the age of information abundance, the thirst for knowledge paradoxically produces distraction. The continual rush of news updates, email notifications, and digital stuff inundates our senses, exhausting our cognitive capacity. The fear of missing out (FOMO) fosters obsessive information intake, creating cycles of distraction and worry.

Psychological Triggers and Attention Hijackers

Behind every distraction is a psychological trigger—a subconscious indication that drives us to shift our attention. From vivid colors and compelling images to sporadic incentives and social approval, digital interfaces are meant to exploit our fundamental weaknesses. Attention hijackers, such as click bait headlines and auto play features, capitalize on our cognitive biases to prolong attention.

The Impact on Mental Well-being

The implications of persistent distraction extend beyond temporary slips in attention. Prolonged exposure to digital distractions corresponds with heightened stress levels, impaired cognitive resilience, and poor general well-being. Our brains, geared for prolonged attention, struggle to adjust to the fragmented stimuli of the digital era, leading to cognitive weariness and burnout.

Cultivating Digital Literacy and Mindful Consumption

Amidst the onslaught of distractions, cultivating digital literacy and practicing mindful consumption emerge as key tactics for restoring attention. By gaining discernment in our online relationships, we can discriminate between real participation and mindless scrolling. Setting purposeful boundaries, such as specified digital detox periods and app usage limitations, helps individuals recover control of their attentional resources.

The Call to Action: Embracing Cognitive Freedom

Understanding current distractions is the first step towards fostering cognitive freedom—the ability to focus our attention purposefully and sustainably. By realizing the omnipresence of distractions and their influence on our lives, we open the way for intentional decisions and purposeful ways to keep our attention despite the cacophony of the digital age.

In the chapters ahead, we will go further into practical approaches and concrete ideas for mastering attention and navigating distractions efficiently. Let us go on this road toward regaining our attention and cultivating cognitive resilience in an era marked by incessant stimulation and digital noise.

This investigation of current distractions offers readers a detailed knowledge of the issues provided by contemporary technology and information overload. It highlights the need for digital literacy and mindful consumption as key skills for resisting distractions and building cognitive well-being.

Chapter 2

The Science of Attention

Attention is a multifaceted cognitive process that allows us to select, focus on, and process specific information while filtering out irrelevant stimuli. In this chapter, we will embark on a journey into the intricate workings of attention, exploring its neurobiological underpinnings, cognitive mechanisms, and practical implications for enhancing focus and concentration.

The Neurobiology of Attention

Attention is orchestrated by a complex interplay of brain regions and neural networks, each contributing to different aspects of attentional control and allocation. At the forefront of attention regulation is the prefrontal cortex, a region responsible for executive functions such as goal-setting, decision-making, and sustained attention. The parietal and temporal lobes play crucial roles in spatial and object-based attention, respectively, while the thalamus acts as a relay station for sensory information.

Neural Pathways and Attentional Networks

Neuroimaging studies have revealed distinct neural pathways associated with different types of attention. The dorsal attention network, comprising the frontal and parietal cortices, facilitates top-down attentional processes, guiding voluntary focus and cognitive control. In contrast, the ventral attention network, anchored in the temporoparietal junction and ventral frontal cortex, responds to salient stimuli and involuntary shifts of attention.

Neurotransmitters and Attention Modulation

Neurotransmitters such as dopamine, norepinephrine, and acetylcholine modulate attentional processes, regulating arousal levels and cognitive vigilance. Dopamine, in particular, plays a pivotal role in reward-based learning and motivation, influencing our propensity to allocate attention towards rewarding stimuli. Deregulation of neurotransmitter systems can disrupt attentional function, contributing to attention-deficit disorders and other cognitive impairments.

The Cognitive Architecture of Attention

From early sensory processing to higher-order cognitive control, attention unfolds through a hierarchical cascade of cognitive processes. Bottom-up attention, driven by sensory inputs and stimulus salience, captures our awareness spontaneously. Top-down attention, guided by internal goals and expectations, enables sustained focus and selective attention amidst competing stimuli.

Models of Attentional Control

Psychological models of attention, such as the spotlight metaphor and the filter theory, provide conceptual frameworks for understanding attentional selection and inhibition. The spotlight model posits attention as a flexible beam that illuminates specific regions of sensory space, enhancing perceptual processing within its focus. The filter theory, on the other hand, suggests that attention acts as a gatekeeper, filtering relevant information while suppressing irrelevant distractions.

Attentional Capacities and Limitations

Despite its remarkable flexibility, attention is subject to inherent limitations and constraints. The concept of attentional capacity refers to the finite resources available for cognitive processing, influencing our ability to multitask and sustain attention over time. Attentional limitations manifest through phenomena such as inattentional blindness, where individuals fail to perceive unexpected stimuli due to attentional focus.

Attentional Control and Cognitive Load

Efficient attentional control hinges on the ability to allocate resources adaptively, optimizing cognitive load based on task demands and environmental cues. Excessive cognitive load, induced by information overload or complex tasks, can overwhelm attentional capacities, leading to errors and diminished performance. Strategic allocation of attentional resources is essential for managing cognitive load and optimizing task performance.

Implications for Focus and Cognitive Enhancement

Understanding the science of attention has profound implications for enhancing focus and cognitive performance. Neuroplasticity, the brain's capacity to reorganize and adapt in response to experience, underscores the potential for attentional training and interventions. Techniques such as mindfulness meditation, cognitive training, and environmental optimization offer promising avenues for strengthening attentional control and combating distractions in everyday life.

Practical Strategies for Attention Management

Drawing from scientific insights, individuals can adopt practical strategies to optimize attentional resources and cultivate sustained focus. These strategies encompass cognitive-behavioral techniques, lifestyle modifications, and technological interventions aimed at promoting mindful attention and cognitive resilience. By harnessing the principles of attentional science, we empower ourselves to navigate the complexities of the modern world with clarity and purpose.

The Mastery of Attention

In conclusion, the science of attention illuminates the intricate interplay between brain function, cognitive processes, and environmental influences. By unraveling the mysteries of attentional control, we gain valuable insights into optimizing focus, enhancing cognitive performance, and fostering mental well-being. As we continue our exploration of attention in subsequent chapters, let us embrace the transformative power of attentional mastery in shaping our lives and achieving our fullest potential.

Brain Mechanics and Focus

The human brain is a marvel of complexity, comprising billions of neurons interconnected through intricate networks. At the heart of our cognitive abilities lies the capacity for attention and focus, orchestrated by specialized brain regions and neurochemical pathways. In this subchapter, we delve deep into the brain mechanics that underpin our ability to sustain attention and concentrate on specific tasks.

Neuroanatomy of Attention

Attentional processes are mediated by a distributed network of brain regions, each contributing to different facets of attention regulation and control. Key areas implicated in attention include:

Prefrontal Cortex (PFC)

Situated behind the forehead, the prefrontal cortex is the seat of executive functions—higher-order cognitive processes responsible for planning, decision-making, and goal-directed behavior. The dorsolateral prefrontal cortex

(DLPFC) plays a pivotal role in maintaining sustained attention and inhibiting distractions, while the ventrolateral prefrontal cortex (VLPFC) is involved in task switching and cognitive flexibility.

Parietal Cortex

The parietal cortex integrates sensory information and allocates spatial attention, enabling us to focus on specific regions of our environment. The intraparietal sulcus (IPS) is particularly crucial for spatial attention, guiding eye movements, and orienting attention toward relevant stimuli.

Temporoparietal Junction (TPJ)

Located at the junction of the temporal and parietal lobes, the TPJ is involved in social cognition and attentional reorienting. It plays a role in detecting unexpected stimuli and redirecting attention in response to salient events.

Thalamus

Acting as a relay station for sensory inputs, the thalamus filters and prioritizes incoming information, directing relevant signals to cortical areas involved in attentional processing.

Anterior Cingulate Cortex (ACC)

The ACC monitors cognitive conflicts and error signals, regulating attentional control based on task demands and performance feedback.

Neural Pathways and Attention Networks

Attentional control is mediated by specialized neural pathways that facilitate communication between brain regions.

Two primary attention networks have been identified:

Dorsal Attention Network (DAN)

The DAN, comprising the frontal and parietal cortices, supports top-down attentional processes—voluntary allocation of attention based on cognitive goals and expectations. It coordinates the spatial and temporal aspects of attention, guiding selective focus and inhibitory control over distractors.

Ventral Attention Network (VAN)

The VAN, anchored in the temporoparietal junction and ventral frontal cortex, responds to salient stimuli and involuntary shifts of attention. It detects behaviorally relevant cues and facilitates orienting responses toward unexpected events.

Neurotransmitters and Attention Modulation

Neurotransmitters play a critical role in modulating attentional states and cognitive performance.

Key neurotransmitter systems implicated in attention include:

Dopamine

Dopamine regulates motivation, reward processing, and cognitive control. It facilitates the salience of rewarding stimuli, influencing our propensity to allocate attention toward novel or rewarding cues.

Norepinephrine

Norepinephrine modulates arousal levels and vigilance, optimizing attentional resources based on environmental demands. It enhances cognitive readiness and responsiveness to task-relevant stimuli.

Acetylcholine

Acetylcholine supports sustained attention and cognitive flexibility, facilitating learning and memory processes. Dysregulation of acetylcholine levels is implicated in attentional disorders such as Alzheimer's disease.

Neural Plasticity and Attention Training

The brain exhibits remarkable plasticity—the ability to reorganize and adapt in response to experience and environmental stimuli. Neuroplasticity underlies the efficacy of attention training interventions, such as mindfulness meditation and cognitive exercises, in sculpting attentional circuits and enhancing cognitive resilience.

Practical Implications for Enhancing Focus

Understanding the brain mechanics of attention has profound implications for optimizing focus and cognitive performance. By leveraging neuroscientific insights, individuals can adopt practical strategies to enhance attentional control:

Mindfulness Meditation

Mindfulness practices cultivate present-moment awareness and attentional stability, fostering sustained focus and emotional regulation.

Cognitive Training

Cognitive exercises targeting attentional functions, such as selective attention and inhibitory control, promote cognitive flexibility and resilience.

Environmental Optimization

Creating an optimal workspace and minimizing distractions enhances attentional engagement and productivity.

Unraveling the Mysteries of Focus

In conclusion, the brain mechanics of attention unveil the intricate interplay between neural circuits, neurotransmitter systems, and cognitive processes underlying focus and concentration. By unraveling these mysteries, we gain invaluable insights into optimizing attentional resources and fostering cognitive well-being. As we embark on our journey towards mastering focus, let us harness the transformative power of neuroscientific knowledge to navigate the complexities of the modern world with clarity and purpose.

Neuroplasticity and Concentration

Neuroplasticity, also known as brain plasticity, refers to the brain's remarkable ability to reorganize itself by forming new neural connections in response to learning, experience, and environmental stimuli. This dynamic process underlies our capacity to adapt, learn new skills, and enhance cognitive functions, including concentration and attention. In this subchapter, we unravel the intricate interplay between neuroplasticity and concentration, exploring how the brain's adaptive mechanisms shape our ability to focus amidst distractions.

The Foundations of Neuroplasticity

Neuroplasticity challenges the long-held notion that the adult brain is fixed and immutable. Instead, research has demonstrated that the brain remains plastic throughout life, continuously reshaping its structure and function in response to internal and external stimuli. At the cellular level, neuroplasticity is driven by synaptic plasticity—the ability of synapses (junctions between neurons) to strengthen or weaken in response to activity patterns.

Hebbian Learning and Synaptic Plasticity

The principles of Hebbian learning—often summarized as "neurons that fire together, wire together"—capture the essence of synaptic plasticity. When neurons repeatedly activate in synchrony, synaptic connections are reinforced, leading to long-lasting changes in neural circuits. This synaptic strengthening underpins the acquisition of new skills and the consolidation of memory traces.

Structural Plasticity and Dendritic Remodeling

Beyond synaptic changes, neuroplasticity encompasses structural modifications within neurons. Dendritic spines, small protrusions on dendrites (branch-like extensions of neurons), undergo dynamic remodeling in response to experience. Learning and practice induce dendritic growth and synaptogenesis, facilitating information processing and connectivity within neural networks.

Neuroplasticity and Learning

Concentration and focus are cognitive skills that rely heavily on neuroplasticity. When we engage in tasks requiring sustained attention, neural circuits associated with attentional control undergo adaptive changes. These neuroplastic changes optimize the efficiency of attentional networks, enhancing our ability to filter out distractions and maintain concentration over time.

Experience-Dependent Plasticity

Experience-dependent plasticity refers to the brain's capacity to reorganize based on specific learning experiences. For instance, musicians exhibit structural changes in auditory regions of the brain, enabling heightened sensitivity to musical nuances. Similarly, individuals who practice meditation show increased cortical thickness in attention-related areas, reflecting neuroplastic adaptations to sustained focus and mindfulness.

Skill Acquisition and Expertise

Skill acquisition is a testament to the transformative power of neuroplasticity. Whether mastering a musical instrument, learning a new language, or honing athletic abilities, repeated practice reshapes neural circuits, optimizing performance and efficiency. Expertise emerges from a combination of deliberate practice and neuroplastic adaptations, refining attentional control and cognitive precision.

Harnessing Neuroplasticity for Concentration

Understanding the principles of neuroplasticity empowers individuals to optimize concentration and attentional focus through targeted interventions:

Cognitive Training Programs

Structured cognitive training programs leverage neuroplasticity to enhance attentional functions. Tasks designed to challenge working memory, inhibitory control, and sustained attention promote adaptive neuroplastic changes, facilitating concentration and cognitive resilience.

Mindfulness Meditation

Mindfulness meditation cultivates neuroplasticity in attention-related brain regions, fostering sustained focus and emotional regulation. Regular practice strengthens neural networks involved in attentional control, enabling individuals to navigate distractions with greater ease.

Environmental Enrichment

Enriched environments promote neuroplasticity by exposing the brain to diverse sensory stimuli and cognitive challenges. By engaging in intellectually stimulating activities and adopting a curiosity-driven mindset, individuals can promote neural growth and optimize concentration.

Neuroplasticity and Cognitive Resilience

Neuroplasticity underscores the brain's capacity for adaptation and resilience in the face of cognitive challenges. By embracing lifelong learning and adopting growth-oriented strategies, individuals can harness the transformative potential of neuroplasticity to sustain concentration, enhance cognitive performance, and cultivate a resilient mind.

The Dynamic Brain

In conclusion, neuroplasticity represents a paradigm shift in our understanding of brain function, highlighting the brain's dynamic capacity for growth and adaptation. By embracing neuroplastic principles, we unlock new possibilities for concentration and cognitive enhancement, harnessing the brain's innate plasticity to navigate the complexities of the modern world with clarity and focus. As we embark on our journey towards mastering concentration, let us celebrate the extraordinary resilience of the human brain and embrace the transformative potential of neuroplasticity in shaping our cognitive destiny.

Chapter 3

The Myth of Multitasking

Multitasking—the seemingly superhuman capacity to handle numerous things simultaneously—has long been lauded as a characteristic of efficiency and productivity. In truth, however, the idea of multitasking masks a basic cognitive mistake. In this chapter, we explore the intricacies of multitasking, refuting prevalent myths and investigating the adverse impacts of task switching on attentional performance and cognitive well-being.

The Illusion of Multitasking

Multitasking is typically seen as a desirable skill—a tribute to one's abilities to handle competing demands and enhance output. The attractiveness of multitasking arises from its seeming efficiency; by tackling numerous activities at once, folks think they can do more in less time. However, under the surface lurks a cognitive illusion—a mirage of productivity that covers the actual costs of split attention.

The Cognitive Costs of Task Switching

At its foundation, multitasking entails fast task switching—shifting attention back and forth between various tasks. Each move incurs a cognitive penalty, known as the "switching cost," which appears as extra time and effort necessary to resume and concentrate on a new activity. The brain grapples with competing demands, fragmenting attention and impairing cognitive performance.

Task-Switching Paradigms

Experimental investigations utilizing task-switching paradigms highlight the cognitive problems faced by multitasking. Participants assigned alternating between two tasks exhibit shorter response times and increased mistake rates compared to concentrated single-task settings. These findings underline the limits of attentional resources when divided among different tasks.

The Fallacy of Multitasking Efficiency

Contrary to common assumptions, multitasking does not boost productivity; rather, it reduces performance across activities. Cognitive overload and attentional fragmentation limit information processing, resulting in lower accuracy and quality of output. What looks like simultaneous task performance is, in reality, a succession of partial engagements—sacrificing depth for breadth.

Continuous Partial Attention (CPA)

Linda Stone invented the term "continuous partial attention" (CPA) to characterize the ubiquitous condition of split attention generated by multitasking. In this state, individuals retain a surface awareness of various inputs without completely engaging with any one job. CPA encourages distractibility and reduces concentration, hindering sustained focus and cognitive engagement.

Cognitive Limitations and Attentional Capacity

Multitasking leverages the brain's finite attentional capacity, pushing cognitive constraints beyond ideal thresholds. The brain's attentional resources are allocated unevenly when divided among activities, resulting in reduced performance and greater mental weariness. This cognitive overload affects decision-making, problem-solving, and creative thinking—essential components of efficient job performance.

Bottlenecks in Information Processing

The brain confronts barriers in information processing during multitasking, impeding effective task completion. When attention is spread among several stimuli, crucial information may be neglected or misconstrued, resulting in mistakes and oversights. The brain struggles to prioritize and deploy resources properly, impairing job prioritization and time management.

The Myth of "Good" Multitaskers

Some persons pride themselves on their perceived proficiency as "good" multitaskers—those competent at juggling numerous jobs with ease. However, evidence reveals that self-professed multitasking skill generally corresponds with inferior performance on cognitive tests. The illusion of multitasking efficiency covers cognitive deficiencies and prevents self-awareness of attentional constraints.

The Cognitive Neuroscience of Task Switching

Neuroscientific investigations reveal the brain processes behind task switching and cognitive control. The prefrontal cortex, particularly the dorsolateral prefrontal cortex (DLPFC), plays a crucial role in executive functioning and attentional control. Task switching involves activation of inhibitory systems to suppress irrelevant inputs and enable cognitive flexibility.

Practical Strategies for Task Management

Debunking the illusion of multitasking means adopting alternate tactics for task management and cognitive optimization:

Single-Tasking and Prioritization

Prioritize tasks based on priority and urgency, paying undivided attention to one activity at a time. Single-tasking encourages deep involvement and boosts knowledge retention, boosting cognitive efficiency and task completion.

Time Blocking and Task Batching

Allocate fixed periods for certain work, limiting distractions and cognitive context-switching. Task batching bundles comparable activities together, improving workflow and lowering the cognitive burden associated with task transitions.

Mindfulness and Attention Training

Practice mindfulness practices to build present-moment awareness and sustained attention. Attention training activities strengthen cognitive control and resilience, helping individuals negotiate distractions with clarity and intention.

Redefining Productivity

In conclusion, the myth of multitasking obscures the fundamental constraints of split attention and task switching. By refuting misunderstandings and embracing targeted task management practices, individuals may maximize cognitive function and productivity. Let us reframe productivity not as the ability to multitask, but as the capacity to engage profoundly with one activity at a time—fostering cognitive clarity, efficiency, and well-being in an era marked by distractions and cognitive overload.

Debunking Multitasking

Multitasking—the concept of concurrently executing numerous tasks—has infiltrated modern work culture as a sign of efficiency and productivity. However, under the surface lurks a cognitive fallacy—a belief that weakens attentional performance and degrades cognitive well-being. In this subchapter, we go on a quest to dispel the myth of multitasking, dissecting its cognitive constraints and exploring evidence-based insights into the harmful impacts of split attention on productivity and mental clarity.

The Illusion of Simultaneous Task Execution

At its foundation, multitasking comprises the contemporaneous execution of many tasks—juggling emails while participating in a meeting, texting while driving, or accessing social media while studying. While this may look efficient on the surface, the truth is significantly more complex. The brain's ability to split attention is finite, subject to cognitive restrictions that inhibit optimal task performance.

Cognitive Switching Costs

Multitasking includes fast task switching—shifting attention back and forth between various tasks. Each changeover incurs a cognitive "switching cost," defined by the increased time and effort necessary to shift between tasks. The brain grapples with competing demands, fragmenting attention and diminishing information processing efficiency.

Task Interference and Performance Decline

Contrary to common assumptions, multitasking does not boost productivity; rather, it reduces performance across activities. Task interference occurs when cognitive resources are distributed unevenly, resulting in mistakes, oversights, and lower task completion rates. What looks like simultaneous task performance is, in reality, a succession of partial engagements—sacrificing depth for breadth.

Cognitive Overload and Information Processing Bottlenecks

Multitasking leverages the brain's limited attentional capacity, pushing cognitive boundaries beyond ideal thresholds. The brain experiences information processing bottlenecks during multitasking, impeding effective task completion and degrading decision-making ability. Critical information may be ignored or misconstrued, resulting in mistakes and lower productivity.

Attentional Fragmentation and Reduced Focus

Divided attention generates attentional fragmentation—a condition of cognitive disorder defined by superficial involvement with several stimuli. Continuous partial attention (CPA) encourages distractibility and inhibits sustained concentration, diminishing cognitive engagement and impeding deep information processing.

The Fallacy of Multitasking Proficiency

Some persons pride themselves on their perceived proficiency as "good" multitaskers—those competent at juggling numerous jobs with ease. However, evidence reveals that self-professed multitasking skill generally corresponds with inferior performance on cognitive tests. The illusion of multitasking efficiency covers cognitive deficiencies and prevents self-awareness of attentional constraints.

Cognitive Costs of Task Switching

Neuroscientific investigations reveal the brain processes behind task switching and cognitive control. The prefrontal cortex, particularly the dorsolateral prefrontal cortex (DLPFC), plays a crucial role in executive functioning and attentional control. Task switching involves activation of inhibitory systems to suppress irrelevant inputs and enable cognitive flexibility.

The "Serial Tasking" Alternative

Debunking the myth of multitasking needs a paradigm change towards targeted task management solutions. Rather than attempting to juggle numerous activities simultaneously, individuals might adopt a "serial tasking" approach—prioritizing tasks based on priority and paying concentrated attention to one task at a time.

Single-Tasking and Deep Work

Single-tasking encourages intense involvement with tasks, boosting knowledge retention and cognitive clarity. By immersing oneself totally in a single task, individuals optimize attentional resources and foster cognitive efficiency. Deep work—the discipline of persistent, undistracted focus—fosters creativity, productivity, and professional success.

Task Prioritization and Time Management

Effective task prioritizing is vital for minimizing the cognitive costs of multitasking. Allocate fixed periods for certain work, limiting distractions and cognitive context-switching. Task batching bundles comparable activities together, improving workflow and lowering cognitive burden associated with task transitions.

The Mindful Approach to Task Management

Mindfulness practices offer a comprehensive approach to controlling attention and boosting cognitive performance. By fostering present-moment awareness and mindfulness, individuals can strengthen attentional control and lessen the influence of distractions on cognitive engagement.

Mindfulness Meditation

Mindfulness meditation teaches attentional abilities and promotes cognitive resilience, helping individuals to negotiate interruptions with clarity and intention. Regular practice develops attentional networks and supports emotional control, boosting general well-being and cognitive flexibility.

Mindful Technology Use

Practice mindful technology usage by creating purposeful limits and reducing digital distractions. Implement "digital detox" intervals and adjust digital settings to encourage focused attention and offset the harmful effects of multitasking.

Redefining Productivity and Cognitive Engagement

In conclusion, exposing the illusion of multitasking demands a reevaluation of productivity and cognitive engagement. By embracing focused task management tactics and prioritizing deep work, individuals may maximize attentional resources and promote cognitive clarity. Let us reframe productivity not as the ability to multitask, but as the capacity to engage completely with one activity at a time—fostering cognitive efficiency, creativity, and well-being in an era marked by distractions and cognitive overload.

The Cost of Task Switching

activity switching—the process of shifting attention from one activity to another—imposes cognitive and productivity costs that can affect performance and well-being. In this subchapter, we analyze the hidden toll of task switching, addressing its neurocognitive causes, practical ramifications, and evidence-based techniques for enhancing attentional concentration and workflow efficiency.

Understanding Task Switching

Task switching happens when individuals change between various tasks or cognitive demands. Each changeover involves a mental effort to withdraw from one activity and reorient towards another, breaking the flow of attention and hindering cognitive function. While appearing benign, frequent task switching takes a severe toll on attentional resources and mental clarity.

Types of Task Switching

Task switching covers several types, including:

- External Task Switching: Shifting emphasis between physical tasks or activities (e.g., replying to emails while attending a conference).
- Internal Task Switching: Transitioning between cognitive activities or mental states (e.g., switching between brainstorming ideas and revising a manuscript).
- Interpersonal Task Switching: Juggling social connections with professional obligations (e.g., engaging in discussions while performing work tasks).

The Cognitive Toll of Task Switching

Task switching incurs cognitive costs that affect attentional control and information processing efficiency. Key cognitive consequences of task switching include:

Switching Costs

Each task changeover entails a "switching cost"—a brief increase in cognitive burden associated with disengagement from one task and activation of cognitive processes necessary for the new one. Switching costs show as delays in job commencement, lower productivity, and heightened mental weariness.

Working Memory Overload

Task switching stresses working memory—a limited-capacity cognitive mechanism responsible for the temporary storage and processing of information. Rapid task transitions drain working memory resources, reducing cognitive flexibility and inhibitory control.

Attentional Fragmentation

Frequent task switching generates attentional fragmentation—a condition of fragmented attention characterized by superficial involvement with many stimuli. Continuous partial attention (CPA) impairs sustained concentration and limits deep information processing, impairing task performance and decision-making.

Productivity Implications of Task Switching

Task switching exacts a significant toll on productivity, weakening efficiency and workflow effectiveness. Key productivity consequences of task switching include:

Reduced Task Completion Rates

Task switching reduces task completion rates by lengthening task durations and adding delays associated with cognitive shifts. The cumulative impact of switching costs degrades productivity and hampers goal accomplishment.

Increased Error Rates

Frequent task switching boosts mistake rates by disturbing attentional concentration and compromising information processing accuracy. Errors originating from task switching weaken task quality and need remedial measures, further draining cognitive resources.

Impaired Cognitive Flexibility

Chronic task switching impedes cognitive flexibility—the capacity to adaptively shift attentional focus and mental processes. Reduced cognitive flexibility hampers adaptive problem-solving and impairs creative thinking, hurting innovation and professional advancement.

Neurocognitive Mechanisms of Task Switching

Task switching activates distinct neurocognitive systems inside the brain, including:

Prefrontal Cortex Activation

The prefrontal cortex, particularly the dorsolateral prefrontal cortex (DLPFC), plays a crucial role in executive functioning and cognitive regulation. Task switching involves activation of inhibitory systems to suppress irrelevant inputs and enable cognitive flexibility.

Neurotransmitter Modulation

Neurotransmitters such as dopamine and norepinephrine regulate attentional processes and arousal levels during task switching. Dysregulation of neurotransmitter systems relates to attentional deficits and cognitive impairments associated with persistent task switching.

Neural Network Adaptations

Chronic task switching promotes adaptive alterations within brain networks linked with attentional regulation and information processing. Structural and functional modifications remodel brain circuits, altering task performance and cognitive resilience.

Strategies for Mitigating Task-Switching Costs

Optimizing attentional concentration and workflow efficiency includes adopting evidence-based solutions for minimizing task-switching costs:

Prioritize Task Sequencing

Sequence tasks depending on cognitive demands and attentional requirements, minimizing abrupt transitions between activities. Prioritize complicated, intellectually demanding tasks during moments of maximal attention and energy.

Implement Time-Blocking Techniques

Allocate fixed time periods for certain work, limiting distractions and cognitive context-switching. Time blocking optimizes task continuity and encourages prolonged attentional involvement.

Minimize External Distractions

Create an ideal work environment by limiting external distractions and maximizing workstation ergonomics.

Implement digital detox intervals and create clear limits to reduce the influence of external stimuli on attentional concentration.

Practice Mindful Task Management

Embrace mindfulness practices to build present-moment awareness and sustained attention. Practice mindful task management by setting purposeful aims and sustaining cognitive clarity among distractions.

Real-World Applications and Examples

Consider the following real-world examples to demonstrate the practical consequences of task-switching costs:

- Professional Context: A project manager juggles numerous responsibilities concurrently, typically jumping between team meetings, client interactions, and project planning. Task switching affects decision-making and limits effective resource allocation, resulting in project delays and lower productivity.

- Academic Setting: A student attempts to multitask while studying, alternating between reading course materials, monitoring social media alerts, and drafting emails. Task switching weakens knowledge retention and limits deep learning, affecting academic achievement and impairing exam preparation.

Optimizing Attentional Focus and Workflow Efficiency

In conclusion, the cost of task switching underlines the cognitive and productivity consequences of split attention and frequent cognitive transitions. By understanding the neurocognitive principles underpinning task switching and implementing evidence-based solutions for minimizing switching costs, people may enhance attentional concentration and workflow efficiency. Let us prioritize cognitive clarity and attentive task management, supporting productivity and well-being in an era marked by distractions and cognitive overload.

Chapter 4

The Power of Deep Work

In an era marked by continual connectivity and digital distractions, the capacity to engage in deep, concentrated work has become an uncommon and valued talent. Deep work—the act of immersing oneself in cognitively challenging activities with continuous focus and minimum distractions—holds substantial implications for productivity, creativity, and personal fulfillment. In this chapter, we examine the transforming impact of deep work, uncovering evidence-based insights and practical tactics for building deep work habits in pursuit of cognitive clarity and professional greatness.

Defining Deep Work

Deep work, popularised by Cal Newport in his seminal book "Deep Work: Rules for Focused Success in a Distracted World," refers to tasks performed in a state of distraction-free concentration that stretches cognitive skills to their maximum. Deep work is characterized by:

- Cognitive Depth: Engaging in tasks that involve significant attention, innovative problem-solving, and cognitive engagement.
- Undivided Attention: Immersing oneself totally in a single activity, limiting interruptions and external distractions.

- Meaningful Output: Producing high-quality work that displays cognitive effort and knowledge of subject matter.

The Benefits of Deep Work

Cultivating deep work habits gives a range of benefits across personal and professional domains:

Enhanced Productivity and Efficiency

Deep work maximizes cognitive resources, enabling individuals to do more in less time. By decreasing task-switching and attentional fragmentation, deep work promotes workflow efficiency and task completion rates.

Improved Cognitive Performance

Engaging in serious work supports cognitive growth and skill improvement. Deeply concentrated activities induce brain plasticity, boosting information processing, memory consolidation, and problem-solving ability.

Increased Creativity and Innovation

Deep work encourages creative discoveries and creativity by promoting prolonged attention and varied thinking. Uninterrupted engagement in challenging work enhances cognitive flexibility and unlocks creative potential.

Professional Mastery and Expertise

Regular practice of deep work cultivates competence and mastery within specialised fields. Deeply engaged activities enhance skill growth and competence, enabling individuals to reach professional greatness.

The Neuroscience of Deep Work

Neuroscientific research reveals the cognitive factors driving deep labor and focused attention:

Prefrontal Cortex Activation

Deep work involves the prefrontal cortex, particularly the dorsolateral prefrontal cortex (DLPFC), responsible for executive functioning and cognitive control. Activation of the DLPFC enhances sustained attention, inhibitory control, and goal-directed behavior.

Default Mode Network Suppression

Deep work suppresses the default mode network (DMN)—a brain network involved with mind-wandering and self-referential contemplation. DMN suppression boosts cognitive concentration and promotes task-relevant neuronal activations.

Neuroplasticity and Skill Acquisition

Regular involvement in intense labor generates neuroplastic alterations within brain networks linked with skill learning and information processing. Structural and functional adaptations boost cognitive performance and allow expertise acquisition.

Strategies for Cultivating Deep Work

Optimizing deep work needs careful practice and strategic deployment of concentrated work habits:

Establish Rituals and Routines

Create rituals and habits to indicate intensive work times and limit distractions. Designate a discrete workstation, create precise time blocks for intensive work, and avoid digital distractions.

Prioritize Cognitive Depth

Identify tasks that need deep cognitive involvement and prioritize them during moments of peak attention and energy. Allocate unbroken time chunks for complicated, mentally demanding activities.

Embrace Solitude and Silence

Seek seclusion and stillness to develop intense focus and mental immersion. Minimize external stimulation and create a suitable atmosphere for continuous cognitive engagement.

Practice Attention Training

Develop attentional abilities through mindfulness meditation and attention training activities. Cultivate present-moment awareness and strengthen cognitive control to retain attention among distractions.

Real-World Applications of Deep Work

Consider the following real-world instances to demonstrate the practical consequences of deep work:

- Professional Development: A software engineer dedicates uninterrupted time blocks to challenging coding jobs, creating breakthroughs in software development, and enhancing code efficiency.
- Academic Excellence: A researcher immerses oneself in long work sessions to evaluate data and create research articles, creating intellectual depth and contributing to scientific growth.
- Creative Endeavors: An artist embraces serious labor to explore new artistic approaches and make significant artworks, surpassing creative boundaries and stimulating artistic innovation.

Embracing Deep Work

In an era marked by continual connectivity and digital distractions, adopting deep work—a state of focused, undistracted attention on cognitively challenging tasks—holds substantial implications for productivity, creativity, and cognitive clarity. In this subchapter, we dig into the fundamentals of deep work, revealing evidence-based tactics and practical advice for building deep work habits and maximizing cognitive function despite current hurdles.

Understanding the Essence of Deep Work

Deep work covers actions performed in a state of distraction-free concentration that pushes cognitive skills to their maximum. Key features of deep work include:

- Cognitive Depth: Engaging in tasks that involve significant attention, innovative problem-solving, and cognitive engagement.
- Sustained Attention: Immersing oneself totally in a single task, limiting interruptions and external distractions.
- Meaningful Output: Producing high-quality work that displays cognitive effort and knowledge of subject matter.

The Benefits of Embracing Deep Work

Embracing deep labor gives a range of advantages across personal and professional domains:

Enhanced Productivity and Task Efficiency

Deep work maximizes cognitive resources, enabling individuals to do more in less time. By decreasing task-switching and attentional fragmentation, deep work promotes workflow efficiency and task completion rates.

Improved Cognitive Performance and Skill Development

Engaging in serious work increases cognitive growth and skill gain. Deeply concentrated activities induce brain plasticity, boosting information processing, memory consolidation, and problem-solving ability.

Enhanced Creativity and Innovation

Deep work encourages creative discoveries and creativity by promoting prolonged attention and varied thinking. Uninterrupted engagement in challenging work enhances cognitive flexibility and unlocks creative potential.

Professional Mastery and Expertise Development

Regular practice of deep work cultivates competence and mastery within specialised fields. Deeply engaged activities enhance skill growth and competence, enabling individuals to reach professional greatness.

Strategies for Embracing Deep Work

Optimizing deep work needs careful practice and strategic deployment of concentrated work habits:

Create a Deep Work Ritual

Establish a regular ritual or habit to signify intensive work sessions. Designate a discrete workstation, create precise time limits for intensive work, and avoid digital distractions.

Example: Renowned author and computer science professor Cal Newport highlights the necessity of building a meaningful work ritual to increase cognitive engagement and productivity. Newport's ritual comprises a defined workplace, set work hours, and purposeful avoidance of non-essential duties during serious work sessions.

Prioritize Tasks Based on Importance and Cognitive Demand

Identify tasks that need deep cognitive involvement and prioritize them during moments of peak attention and energy. Allocate unbroken time chunks for complicated, mentally demanding activities.

Example: A software engineer prioritizes deep work sessions for coding and problem-solving activities, arranging uninterrupted time blocks to handle hard technical challenges and enhance software development.

Embrace Solitude and Silence

Seek seclusion and stillness to develop intense focus and mental immersion. Minimize external stimulation and create a suitable atmosphere for continuous cognitive engagement.

Example: A researcher immerses oneself in long work sessions in a quiet, secluded workstation to analyze data, prepare research articles, and develop unique scientific ideas.

Practice Attention Training and Mindfulness

Develop attentional abilities through mindfulness meditation and attention training activities. Cultivate present-moment awareness and strengthen cognitive control to retain attention among distractions.

Example: A corporate leader integrates mindfulness techniques into their daily routine, practicing meditation to promote mental clarity and resilience in high-pressure work conditions.

Techniques for profound focus

Twice a year, Microsoft co-founder Bill Gates retires to a cottage in the woods to do nothing but read and contemplate big things. During his self-proclaimed "think weeks," Gates entirely isolates himself from the outer world—meaning no email, no phone calls, and no internet access. It's just him and a stack of papers from Microsoft workers selling new inventions or investments.

Gates fully removes distractions from his environment to prioritize deep work—a level of concentration that promotes creativity and attention. And it worked, as work done during Gates' "think weeks" resulted in inventions like the debut of Internet Explorer in 1995.

But you don't have to go to a wooded lodge to reap the full advantages of deep work. While most of us don't have the luxury of moving away for days or weeks at a time, you can still weave deep work into your everyday routine with a few easy habits.

What is deep work?

Deep work is a condition of peak focus that allows you to learn hard topics and accomplish great work rapidly. The term was invented by Cal Newport, a computer science professor at Georgetown University and author of "Deep Work: Rules for Focused Success in a Distracted World." In his book, Newport describes deep work as a state of distraction-free concentration when your brain functions at its greatest capacity.

Simply expressed, Newport's deep work theory says that to be genuinely productive, we should log out of all communication tools and work, uninterrupted, for significant periods every day. So although you might not be able to entirely break away from your team communication tools, strive for 60-90 distraction-free minutes at a time.

Deep vs. "shallow" work

Newport describes shallow work as logistical-style jobs that can be completed while distracted, such as work coordination and communication chores that are easy to reproduce.

At Asana, we call this "work about work." According to our research, 60% of knowledge workers' time is spent on coordination activities like answering emails, planning projects, and arranging meetings. And while it's not possible to eliminate all shallow labor from most occupations, reducing time spent on shallow work can generate space for the high-impact tasks that matter most.

The benefits of intense work

Deep work is helpful for two reasons: it helps you avoid distractions and rewires your brain to help you learn hard things faster—so you can get better work done in less time. Here's how:

Deep work helps you avoid distractions

Eliminating distractions is a basic component of deep work, and for good reason. When you flip between tasks—like checking your phone while composing a project proposal—a part of your attention is locked on the preceding work. So even when you go back to writing, a part of your brain is still thinking about that text message you just saw. This condition is called attention residue, and it takes a major toll. Research reveals that it can take upwards of 20 minutes to restore momentum after an interruption—so if you check your phone twice in an hour, that's two-thirds of your concentration time gone.

Deep work rewires your brain

Deep work is the greatest approach to mastering new abilities rapidly. When you focus intently, your brain cements learning pathways and improves the connections between neurons so they can fire quicker. That means when you focus intensively on a certain talent, you're physically rewriting your brain to help you do that skill more efficiently. Furthermore, research shows that this rewiring can only happen when you concentrate on a single job at a time while avoiding distraction (in other words, when you work profoundly).

Why is deep work important?

The ability to work profoundly doesn't simply provide you an edge in the modern workplace—it also brings joy and significance to your everyday responsibilities. Here's how deep work may increase your work performance and enrich your daily life:

It boosts work quality

When you work intensely, you can master tough subjects and deliver great work quickly—two abilities that may put you (and your team) up for success in the modern workplace.

- Learn hard things fast: Learning is an essential aspect of every profession, no matter your sector. For example, an IT manager has to learn how to troubleshoot technology at an organizational size, an accountant needs to learn about tax legislation, and a software engineer needs to master new programming languages. In that manner, the capacity to learn new talents via intense study makes you a valuable asset.
- Create quality work at speed: Learning new abilities is one thing, and creating excellent outcomes is another. This second attribute of deep work lets you employ your skills to make a good effect. For

example, intense focus might assist a project manager in understanding how to write a project proposal, and then construct an in-depth proposal that helps gain financing for a new endeavor.

It's rare

According to our analysis, 60% of knowledge workers' time is spent on coordinating rather than the specialised, strategic duties they were paid to undertake. This propensity towards superficial work instead of actual productivity creates an opportunity for teams who value attention at work because they can achieve greater outcomes than their rivals.

Even while profound work is rare, it doesn't have to be. There are specific actions you can do to assist your team work deeply, including unblocking their time-consuming chores, clarifying work priorities, and enhancing team visibility. If you haven't already, make sure you're:

- Setting communication norms.
- Streamlining work in a single tool.
- Scheduling meetings with forethought.

It feels good

Deep work is more than a method to be more productive—it also just feels wonderful to accomplish. That's because deep work is a form of flow state, a cognitive zone that's innately gratifying and delivers an optimum balance between abilities and challenge.

As a bonus, concentrating intently helps you put value into the world and create things that matter, which in turn may provide a new level of joy to your professional life. Neurological research reveals that your perspective of the world is impacted by what you pay attention to—so if you spend time working intently, your mind interprets your surroundings as full of purpose and value.

A profound life is a good life. "

7 strategies to bring deep work into your schedule

Your mind is like a muscle, which means you may improve your capacity for deep work via exercise and consistency over time. To get you started, we've written out seven guidelines to help you build a deep work habit.

1. Choose a profound work philosophy

To work intensely, you need a strategy that meets your specific schedule and work preferences. In his book, Newport describes four possible ways (or "philosophies") to follow when you select how to arrange your deep work. Depending on your lifestyle, certain ways may work better than others:

- Rhythmic philosophy: With this technique you build a regular habit and rhythm for serious work, blocking aside 1-4 hour chunks to focus at the same time every day. When scheduling time for deep work, bear in mind that most people can't sustain more than four deep work hours per day. For example, you may set time for intensive work between 8-10 am every weekday. The key to this method is consistency, which you may attain by committing to a set amount of serious work every day. To properly use this method, attempt a time management technique that supports it, such time blocking.

- Journalistic philosophy: This technique is the most flexible and allows you to incorporate serious work whenever you can into your schedule. For example, you may arrange time for intense work when you have at least 90 minutes between meetings. Keep in mind that this strategy needs you to transition into deep work mode at will, which might be challenging for novices. If you're just starting and have a set meeting schedule, the rhythmic philosophy may be your best choice.
- Monastic philosophy: With this method, you fully eliminate or dramatically minimize shallow work across all facets of your life. For example, science fiction writer Neal Stephenson notably avoids email and speaking engagements so he may free up brain space for writing. That means Stephenson is virtually tough to get a hold of yet highly productive, having over 80 works to his name. If you want to incorporate a monastic attitude at work, consider time management tools that limit work about work, such as the GTD approach.

- Bimodal philosophy: This strategy includes splitting your time, with lengthy chunks (at least a full day) set aside for intensive work and the rest allocated to everything else. Bimodal scheduling is a more flexible form of the monastic philosophy—instead of fully abandoning superficial labor, you can spend a day or more working intensely and then return to your other duties. An excellent example would be the "think weeks" we described at the beginning when Bill Gates escapes to a lodge in the woods twice a year to read and brainstorm. At Asana, we execute our version of the bimodal idea by supporting No Meeting Wednesday—a whole day for our team members to plunge into work uninterrupted.

If I manage my life in such a manner that I obtain plenty of long, continuous, uninterrupted time chunks, I can write books. But when those parts are divided and fractured, my productivity as a novelist declines spectacularly."

—AUTHOR NEIL STEPHENSON, FROM HIS ESSAY "WHY I AM A BAD CORRESPONDENT"

2. Create rituals that boost your attention

Research reveals that our brains recall unique relationships. When you couple two things—like salt and pepper, or a tidy desk and concentration—your mind learns and anticipates that similar combination in the future. That means you may establish rituals that induce concentration and inform your brain it's time to focus. For example, if you routinely wipe up your desk before writing, a clear workplace will make it simpler for you to focus on writing in the future.

As you design your deep work routine, ask yourself the following questions:

- Where will you work? Consider the setting you'll create—for example, you may work in your office with the door locked and the desk wiped off.
- When and how long will you work? For example, you may opt to work first thing in the morning for 90 minutes before taking a coffee break.
- How will you work? Determine guidelines to direct your attention, such as whether you'll use the internet, how many words you'll write every 20 minutes, or where you'll leave your phone.
- How will you support your work? Make sure you have the items you need arranged beforehand—like reference sheets, coffee, or food.

You may also include extra triggers into your routine to restart your attention, such as lighting a candle, listening to a certain style of music, or dressing in a certain way.

3. Prioritize your highest-impact work

With focus, prioritizing is crucial. Often the more you attempt to do, the less you accomplish—so to work thoroughly, you need to concentrate on the most important assignment and dismiss everything else. Here's how to do it:

- Decide in advance what you'll work on during each intense work session. To work intensely you need to focus on one job and disregard everything else. When you pick what to concentrate on in advance, you may prevent multitasking. And if you receive new requests during your concentration time, there will be less pressure to switch jobs immediately away. Try adopting a prioritizing technique to discover and handle your most critical to-do's, such as the Eisenhower decision matrix, Pareto principle, or eat-the-frog strategy.
- Create clarity with team and corporate goals. Clear objectives are like a compass since they direct your decisions and inform you which chores are most essential. For example, if your team's quarterly objective is based on remodeling your company website, you may more easily de-prioritize enhancement requests for your app. Be careful you adopt a goal-setting framework to make your objectives quantifiable and explicit, such as the SMART goal approach or Objectives and Key Results (OKRs).

4. Track where you spend your time

You need to devote time to get things done, and serious work is no different. That's why controlling your calendar and taking care of your time is critical—because to add more deep work into your routine, you have to make a place for it.

Here are some techniques to help you understand and manage your time:

- Audit how you're spending your work time. Before you can cut away superficial work to make room for deeper activities, you have to understand the sort of work you perform on a day-to-day basis. To accomplish this, note out every activity or task you engage in—then measure the depth of every activity so you know how much time you're spending on deep work vs. superficial work.
- Audit your meetings. Make a list of every work meeting you attend, and evaluate how beneficial it truly is on a scale of 1-5. You may also note how much you pay attention at the meeting if there are frequently action items, and if there's a pre-set agenda. That way, you can judge which sessions are genuinely fruitful, and which would be better as an asynchronous update.
- Schedule your day. Take command of your daily calendar by designating blocks of time for each item you wish to do. Two typical techniques to achieve this are timeboxing and time blocking. Timeboxing is a time-management approach in which you

estimate the amount of time an activity will take and box out time to finish it. The notion of time blocking is similar—but instead of boxing off time for a particular activity, you bundle comparable activities together and accomplish them all in one-time block. Timeboxing is an excellent alternative for scheduling significant work, while time blocking may help you tackle lots of minor activities in one go, like answering emails.

5. 5Reduce digital distractions

Distraction is the arch-nemesis of depth. But distraction—especially of the digital variety—is more widespread than ever in today's fast-paced work environment. At a time when 80% of knowledge workers report working with their inbox open and almost three in four professionals feel pushed to multitask every day, avoiding digital temptations might seem practically impossible.

But limiting distractions is still feasible with a few easy strategies:

- Turn off notifications. Sounds, ads, and notifications flashing across your screen have a detrimental influence on attention and can rapidly startle you out of serious work. When you're attempting to focus, utilize Do Not Disturb mode or snooze notifications for your phone and any communication applications you use. Or to detach, shut out of email and chat programs. Remember that you may always check alerts during your next attention break.

- Make depth your default. That means instead of living in a distracted state and pulling your brain into attention mode to finish things, plan focus breaks—times when you allow yourself to take a breather and give in entirely to distractions. You can utilize this method at your employment or in your personal life. For example, you may arrange a concentration break after work when you're permitted to access the internet and look through social media—then devote your complete attention to making dinner, watching a movie, or conversing with loved ones.
- Choose your tools wisely. According to our study, the average knowledge worker changes between 10 applications 25 times per day to conduct their job—and employees who bounce between apps are also more likely to struggle with successfully prioritizing their work. But just because a tool exists doesn't mean you have to utilize it. Instead of distributing work across several separate applications, carefully pick a project management solution that interacts with all of your business tools, so you have a central source of truth for all of your information. That way, instead of working out of many applications, you can track crucial information in one spot.

6. Schedule time to recharge

Rest is equally as crucial as labor. Setting aside time to recharge every day can help prevent burnout and keep your deep work habits sustainable. Newport says that you should withdraw totally from work to make the most of your downtime, so defining clear limits is crucial. He advocates having a strict cut-off time for work each day (for him, it's 5:30 pm), and avoiding work on the weekends. That means once you're done, you're done—no checking Slack on your phone, preparing emails in your thoughts or worrying about forthcoming meetings.

If it's hard for you to disconnect, try designing a "shut-down procedure" that you follow after each workday. This may be 10-20 minutes when you take a last glance at your email to ensure you're not missing crucial alerts, plan how you'll do any outstanding chores, and review your calendar for the next day. This approach gives peace of mind as you sign off for the day, so you can avoid nagging thoughts about incomplete work.

7. Track progress towards your goals

Setting specific goals is one of the greatest strategies to stay motivated and continue your deep work habits over time. When psychologists investigated the influence of numerous motivating approaches on group performance, they found goal setting was one of the most successful. That's because objectives promote intrinsic motivation—the urge to accomplish that comes from within yourself, rather than external stimuli like praise or reward.

To build a habit of intense work, set short-term objectives to measure metrics like how many hours you wish to focus on each day. Newport proposes constructing a scoreboard where you can log your daily hours and mark off each target you've completed. You may also construct higher-level long-term objectives to help you build up to a specific amount of hours over time—for example, you might start with one hour each day, and then work up to four hours over three months. Just remember to make your objectives quantifiable and explicit with a framework like the SMART goal technique or Objectives and Key Results (OKRs).

Chapter 5

Mindfulness and Meditation

Cultivating Unbroken Attention

In the quest for profound work and persistent cognitive engagement, fostering uninterrupted attention is vital. Mindfulness and meditation activities offer significant tools for training the mind, increasing cognitive clarity, and encouraging sustained attention despite distractions. In this chapter, we dig into the transformational potential of mindfulness and meditation, investigating their neuroscientific basis, practical applications, and significant implications for enhancing attentional concentration and mental well-being.

The Essence of Mindfulness and Meditation

Mindfulness and meditation are contemplative practices based on ancient traditions, stressing present-moment awareness and non-judgmental acceptance of sensory impressions. Key characteristics of mindfulness and meditation include:

- Attention Regulation: Cultivating the capacity to direct and sustain attention on a chosen object of concentration (e.g., breath, sensations, thoughts).

- Emotional Regulation: Developing serenity and resilience in response to internal and external stimuli, enabling emotional balance and well-being.

- Cognitive Flexibility: Enhancing adaptability and mental agility via introspective awareness and non-reactive monitoring of mental processes.

The Neuroscience of Mindfulness and Meditation

Neuroscientific research reveals the neuroplastic impacts of mindfulness and meditation on brain structure and function:

- Default Mode Network (DMN) Modulation: Mindfulness techniques inhibit the DMN—a brain network involved with mind-wandering and self-referential thought—promoting focused attention and cognitive clarity.

- Prefrontal Cortex Activation: Meditation practices engage the prefrontal cortex, particularly the anterior cingulate cortex (ACC) and dorsolateral prefrontal cortex (DLPFC), increasing executive processes and attentional control.

- Neurotransmitter Regulation: Mindfulness practices alter neurotransmitter systems (e.g., serotonin, dopamine), enhancing emotional regulation and stress resilience.

Practical Applications of Mindfulness and Meditation

Integrating mindfulness and meditation into daily activities supports the growth of uninterrupted attention and cognitive clarity:

- Mindful Breathing: Engage in concentrated breathing techniques to anchor attention and control physiological arousal. Notice sensations connected with each breath, increasing present-moment awareness and relaxing the mind.
- Body Scan Meditation: Conduct systematic body scan meditations to strengthen somatic awareness and promote mind-body connection. Observe bodily sensations without judgment, supporting relaxation and stress reduction.

- Focused Attention Meditation: Practice focused attention meditation by concentrating attention on a specific object (e.g., candle flame, mantra). Cultivate prolonged attention and mental stability, boosting cognitive focus and lowering distractibility.
- Open Monitoring Meditation: Engage in open-monitoring meditation by watching thoughts, emotions, and sensations as they emerge without attachment or aversion. Foster meta-awareness and cognitive flexibility, encouraging non-reactive monitoring of mental processes.

Real-World Implications of Mindfulness and Meditation

Consider the following real-world events to show the practical uses of mindfulness and meditation:

- Workplace Well-being: A business executive adds mindfulness techniques into everyday routines, decreasing stress levels and increasing decision-making abilities amidst high-pressure circumstances.
- Academic Excellence: A student combines meditation techniques into study sessions, enhancing attention and memory retention during exam preparation.

- Creativity and Innovation: An entrepreneur adopts mindfulness techniques to nurture creative insights and problem-solving talents, boosting innovation and strategic thinking in business efforts.

Meditation Practices for Enhanced Concentration

This modern, digital-centric society in which we live has made our lives busier than ever, with an unlimited amount of distractions making it increasingly difficult to retain focus on the things that matter. Moreover, in a culture that's intrinsically oriented on high productivity and success, there are often numerous things constantly competing for our attention, impeding our capacity to immerse entirely in the present moment.

On the surface, multitasking might provide the idea of doing more, but it doesn't make you as productive as you believe; in fact, research reveals working on numerous projects at once diminishes attention and productivity by as much as 40 percent . So how do you train your mind to acquire laser-sharp attention on one item at a time?

Meditation is one such approach to boost attention and increase productivity, making it simpler to fulfill your objectives and prioritize activities. So if you're seeking practical techniques to promote mental clarity and boost attention, then this article will give you pause for thinking. Keep reading to find the finest meditations for focus.

How Does Meditation Increase Concentration?

According to a study by Harvard University, the mind is generally distracted in thoughts about anything other than the work at hand roughly 47 percent of the time . Don't get us wrong, we're partial to a fantasy or two to provide us some reprieve from life's constant stressors, but there is such a thing as too much of a good thing.

Focused meditation can assist lengthen your attention span so you can remain concentrated for extended durations of time. Once you learn to be present, concentrating on things for extended durations becomes less tough as the brain's capacity to control impulses subsequently improves.

Several investigations have verified this notion, including research on youngsters with Attention Deficit Disorder (ADD) who learned to meditate. The exercise decreased symptoms of inattentiveness, hyperactivity, and impulsiveness by 50 per cent, with brain scans demonstrating substantial brain changes in individuals. These outcomes were on par with the success of prescription drugs used to treat ADD .

Research reveals that 10 minutes of daily meditation can produce physical changes in the brain, altering how it operates in as little as eight weeks through a process called neuroplasticity. But what precisely does this mean?

The brain communicates through electrical nerve cells called neurons. These brain connections continuously adjust to your surroundings, behavior, and lifestyle; essentially, how you think and feel reorganizes established neural networks. Therefore, constantly teaching the mind to pay attention to the current moment creates new neural connections for concentration, consequently causing structural changes in the brain, including increased grey matter density.

Grey matter is the tissue that composes neuronal cell bodies and is important for functions such as muscular control, sensory perception, emotion, memory, and self-regulation. Furthermore, by thickening the pre-frontal cortex, meditation promotes skills including awareness, focus, decision-making, and cognitive performance .

Communication happens between neurons through electrical brainwaves, all of which resonate at a specific frequency, ranging from slow to rapid. The five basic types of brain frequencies are delta, theta, alpha, beta, and gamma. Meditation helps you to change the frequency of your brainwaves to construct your lived experience.

Beta brainwaves, for instance, are prevalent during concentration, talking, and focused on a certain topic. Practicing concentrated meditation heightens beta brain wave levels, so enhancing the brain's power to control where attention is directed for continuous durations.

In fact, one assessment of 23 trials indicated that even very inexperienced meditators had an increased capacity to avoid distractions while focusing on specific tasks. At the same time, more experienced individuals demonstrated a strong capacity to retain concentration for unusually extended durations.

Types of Meditation to Increase Concentration

Although there are many various styles of meditation, they all have similar end aims: to help you recover attention at any moment of the day, hone in on your goals, and boost productivity.

With that stated, some may be more effective in enhancing focus. See below the numerous contemplative techniques and select the ones that appeal to you.

Mindfulness meditation

The objective of mindfulness meditation is to concentrate entirely on a single focal point, whether it's your breath, feelings in the body, a physical item, or a specific activity. Release any ideas and feelings that occur throughout the procedure without allowing yourself to become engrossed, and then return your attention to your focused point of choice.

By entirely concentrating your attention on a single object, mantra, or sensation, you're essentially training your mind to become oblivious to any distractions, be it internal thoughts and sensations or external stimuli like loud vehicle alarms or people yelling.

Focused breathing meditation

People who have problems concentrating may benefit by counting their breathing cycles. The procedure comprises counting inhale, exhales, one. Inhale, exhale, two. Inhale, exhale, three, and so forth.

Intentionally examine the breath, especially how it flows in and out of the belly. Feel your lungs expanding and contracting. Notice the sensation of air moving in via your nose and out through your mouth. This technique promotes a lasting sense of presence and attention.

Many people may discover that their thoughts have drifted before counting to three; when this happens, go back to one. With persistent effort, you may successfully train your mind to concentrate for increasingly longer durations.

Zen meditation

The purpose of Zen meditation is to manage attention by thinking about not thinking. Rather than focusing on a single object, zen meditation requires a more comprehensive awareness and broad scope of attention that incorporates monitoring subjective impressions, thoughts, and emotions.

An Italian research in 2012 indicated that those who engaged in zen meditation over the long term displayed greater mental stability and a superior capacity to focus .

Practitioners normally take the sitting posture while keeping their eyes semi-open and ignoring any wandering, intrusive, or accidental thoughts that spring up. By training the mind to reach such calm, meditators may reflect on the subject at hand with improved attention and enhanced creativity. Refocus your attention back to your selected focal point.

As a novice, it's advisable to start with short sessions lasting less than five minutes before gradually working your way up to greater durations of time as you get more skilled.

Use guided meditation

Following a guided meditation might be a fantastic approach to keep you on track. Hearing the voice of an instructor directing you through your practice might help keep your thoughts from wandering off.

Use beaded garlands

Beaded rosaries, sometimes known as 'malas', can be a terrific method to help you focus on the work at hand. Place your emphasis on sliding one bead at a time between your fingers with each breath, affirmation, or chant.

Using malas is one of the simplest methods to practice meditation. You may carry your mala with you so it's at hand for when you need it most during your day to keep you aware and in the present.

Choose an appropriate time

When it comes to meditation, there's no right or incorrect time to practice it; it's a fully personal decision depending on your daily routine and temperament. Some people may find that starting their morning with concentrated meditation is great for seizing the day, while others might choose to practice clearing their thoughts before arriving home from work or as part of their peaceful nighttime ritual.

Regardless of the time of day, the time you commit to your meditation must be free from distractions and interruptions to get the most out of your session.

Don't worry about failing

Try not to beat yourself up for failing to focus on your aim consistently; we're all human, and it's natural for our thoughts not to be present 100 percent of the time. Anytime you catch yourself wandering off, respond compassionately to your inner self by expressing thanks for noticing when your attention wanders and guiding yourself back to the present now.

FAQ

How long does it take for meditation to show results?

Studies say it might take up to eight weeks of 10-minute daily meditation sessions for your brain to start reaping the effects. Benefits include greater attention, stronger emotional management, better decision-making, and a boost in memory. Results from meditation in the long run include more efficient communication, greater cognitive function, and heightened drive.

What are you meant to experience when meditating?

Once you've gained some expertise in slowing your jumpy mind and distracting ideas via meditation, you may sense sensations of tranquility, relaxation, completeness, and bliss throughout your session and for a lengthy period afterward. The body might also feel light and airy, free from any strain. This joyful mood enables you to stay concentrated for lengthy durations and better cope with difficult situations.

Should I perform the same meditation every day?

There are several styles of meditation meant to assist you reach different goals. You can attempt different meditation techniques based on the goal you wish to attain as well as what works best for you. Some people may function better by practicing the same meditation daily, while others may benefit from trying new ways. Whatever you select, consistency is always the key.

When should you not perform meditation?

The documented advantages of meditation on mental health are broad, helping to ease symptoms of anxiety, stress, and depression. However, one study indicated that 6 percent of people who exercised mindfulness had unpleasant side effects that lasted more than a month. If meditation increases your sad, upset, or anxious mood, then you should stop and investigate other possibilities for aid.

Chapter 6

Building Focus Habits

What is the Power of Focus?

In today's fast-paced world when we are always on the go and continually overstimulated by technology, it might be tougher than ever to concentrate. However, if you can master the power of attention, you will get more things finished in less time and enhance numerous parts of your life.

Focus implies investing all of your energy and ideas on a certain topic, task, or goal for a set length of time; and no matter how focused you believe you are, there are always methods to improve.

Concentration is a talent, a skill that may be tricky to cultivate at times, but between managing a family, busy work, a commute, my blog, and the other areas of my life over the years; I have established habits and suggestions to enhance concentration.

The objective of this post is to help you increase your attention with little basic exercises that you may practice every day. If you follow these guidelines and work on them little by little you will enhance your attention.

With this new ability of attention, you will have higher self-confidence and stronger willpower and you can achieve your objectives.

Improving attention is a lot like strengthening muscles.

Improving your attention, much like growing stronger, doesn't happen overnight. Instead, you work on it little by little, every day without fail, and you will start to notice changes.

Since having a better health routine will have a favorable influence on other elements of your life, sharpening your concentration will too.

Improved attention improves a broad range of objectives, such as:

- Getting out of debt
- Starting a new company
- Learning a new skill
- Following a regular fitness regimen
- Accomplishing your regular schedule
- Sticking to a diet

Focus is increased by overcoming the transient pain that comes with new tasks and the inevitable obstacles to keeping on track. That's why the strength of concentration is such a vital ability to have.

1. **Avoid Multitasking**

Many of us feel that we are getting more done when we multitask, However, this is not true!

When you attempt to split your concentrate on various activities it nearly always ends up taking more time, and it may be considerably more unpleasant.

When you concentrate on one job at a time it helps you focus and complete more effectively. Also, each time you do a job you will experience a feeling of success that will help you remain inspired for your future ones!

Action Item: Make a "to-do" list and concentrate on getting one item done at a time. Check off each item as you do it and discover that it feels amazing to finish one thing in full and move on to the next!

2. **Eliminate distractions**

Whether you work from home or in the office, it feels like distractions are unlimited, and sometimes it may be fairly tough to find out how not to become sidetracked.

What you need to do to prevent distractions may vary based on what distracts you most, however, you can try some things like:

- Pausing duties
- Wearing headphones with music that helps you concentrate
- Putting your phone on "do not disturb" so you aren't enticed by social media

Action Item: While you are working one day create a note of the things you find yourself becoming distracted by. You may then build techniques to eliminate such distractions while you are working.

3. Use Focused Blocks of Time

Many individuals struggle to stay focused mainly because they have so many different things to accomplish and they feel overwhelmed.

A remedy to this is to split your day and/or work into time blocks when you concentrate, and then take a break. You may have to experiment with whatever works best for you but the Pomodoro Technique is an approach that works for many individuals!

In this strategy you concentrate hard for 25 minutes, take a 5-minute break, then start to work again. After 4 "pomodoros," you may take a longer pause, and so on!

Action Item: Organize your day into time blocks of "focus" and "taking a break" so that you can spend your time properly and get everything done, without burning out too fast!

4. Take pauses between work/study sessions

If you never take a break, there is no way you will be able to keep focused on your job or studies!

Believe it or not, taking pauses during the day may help you accomplish your chores sooner!

People are not machines, therefore it is necessary to take a break, stretch, have good food, grab some water, go for a brief walk, or whatever it is that enables you to reset so you can sit back down and truly concentrate while you are working.

Action Item: Set alarm reminders to ensure you take brief breaks throughout the day so you can concentrate 100% when you are seated and working.

5. Practice mindfulness

Mindfulness simply means that you invest all of your attention and concentration into the item that you are doing at that moment.

For example, when people eat they frequently watch TV or look at their phones, but what we should aim to do is concentrate on our meal. Enjoy it, stop multitasking, and be present in the moment. Be aware.

Small and brief mindfulness exercises, like stretching and concentrating on how your body feels, or sipping on your coffee while doing nothing else but thinking about the smells and fragrances, may assist in sharpening your attention for other daily tasks.

So next time you take a little break, try to be more conscious of the thing you are doing.

Action Item: Use your work or study breaks to cultivate mindfulness. attention totally on what you are doing while you do it, both to sharpen your attention and to give your brain a respite from the hustle and bustle. You may try some of the recommended 5-minute mindfulness exercises here.

6. Think About Your Goals

One of the keys to concentration is keeping your motivation and objectives in mind. If you take the time to truly think deeply about what you want to achieve, it might be a lot simpler to concentrate.

Think about what your success looks like. Think about what it'll take to acquire it. Think about how you feel after you accomplish it.

Can you see it? Can you imagine the feeling of success, the confidence, and the delight you will experience when you reach your goal? Great, because most people don't do that.

And if there's one trick to generating the type of concentration that helps you smash through your difficulties, it's to pretend that you've already accomplished your objective.

Imagine how you would feel, where you would be, what it would look like, and what people would say.

This is the technique to turn your objective from being a dry lifeless wish to a brightly burning want... A desire that'll give you the drive, courage, and mental fortitude to press ahead, no matter how many hurdles come your way.

So, to assist sharpen your attention, you have to acquire the practice of thinking about what you desire — vividly.

Action Item: Close your eyes and think seriously about a goal you wish to attain. Tell yourself that you've ALREADY done it and experience the delight and confidence that it provided you. Keep thinking about the specifics - where you are, who's around you, and what you did to reach this objective.

7. Be Grateful in Advance

Now that you know precisely what you desire, the next stage to building concentration is to be appreciative.

It may seem unusual, but thankfulness helps to increase attention because when you're grateful, you educate your mind to search for the positive in every scenario.

By being appreciative, you are concentrating on your current circumstances. You also become more aware of your existing opportunities and of the individuals around you that may assist you attain your objective. Lastly, being thankful for what you have today helps you recognize what measures you need to take to attain your objective.

Gratitude helps to increase concentration because when you're thankful, you teach your mind to search for the positive in every scenario.

Think about it, those who are successful and have reached their objectives did not do it by moaning and feeling sorry for themselves.

So, get in the practice of being appreciative. Be appreciative of your struggles. Be appreciative of where you are in the process. Be appreciative of your setbacks. Be appreciative of the people in your life.

When you're glad and appreciative your mind will start noticing possibilities that it did not perceive previously.

So be in the habit of being appreciative of your objective before you've attained it. It will assist enhance your attention since you're teaching your brain to be optimistic no matter what.

Action Item: Think about 3 things that you're glad for right now. To make it even more beneficial, think of 3 challenges you're experiencing and write reasons why you're thankful for them. If you need some inspiration you might check out these Things to be Thankful For.

8. Be Ruthless With Your Time

Ruthlessly eliminate out "fluff" work and concentrate on the core actions required to attain your objectives - outsource everything else.

The easiest method to achieve this is to create a to-do list that you actively work on every single day.

It might be especially pleasant to put down your to-do list on a Post-it note so you can physically cross off activities as you finish them!

But there are many online to-do list applications on your phone you can use to help you be more ruthless with your time.

The objective is that you want to be intentional with your time and concentrate your attention on the tasks stated on your to-do list. Don't allow distractions or other last-minute things to drag you off target unless they are on your to-do list.

By planning out your day, you are boosting your concentration on the critical activities that you've specified for yourself ahead of time, rather than allowing distractions to sneak up on and steal your attention.

Action Item: Being ruthless with your time involves prioritizing tasks and selecting what is worth your time, and what isn't. You may utilize the Eisenhower Matrix to assist you make judgments about when you should do things, or whether you should do them at all.

By organizing items into a matrix of 4 categories: Urgent, Not Urgent, Important, and Not Important, you may determine what you 1) Do first 2) Plan 3) Delegate 4) or Delete all out. You may find information on the Eisenhower Matrix here!

9. Create "Layers" of Focus

Do the simple things and follow it up with tougher stuff. The sense of success and confidence will boost your attention - not diminish it. Things like:

- ➢ making your bed
- ➢ returning phone calls
- ➢ clearing away junk mail

Doing these low-effort activities helps you feel more successful and is a strong visual indication when you notice that your to-do list has items knocked off it. You have done things, and this boosts your concentration!

This is another reason why having a to-do list is so crucial! Put a few low-effort activities first and then your big goals later, so you may gain the sensation of achievement and a boost of self-confidence to keep motivated and focused throughout the day.

Action Item: Right now, do the tasks on your to-do list that would take no more than two minutes to do. Just get them done – now! You will see how good it feels.

10. Pay Attention to HOW You're Eating

Many of us eat too much and too quickly.

Be attentive and present while you eat. Sit down, chew slowly, appreciate the flavors, and simply enjoy your food. This will help you feel more full and more content with your meals. This makes eating more pleasant and may even help you lose weight!

This is a basic strategy that my wife employs as a nutritionist to help her clients feel more full and more content after a meal.

The tricky thing is that by concentrating on this mindful eating you also increase your general attention.

Action Item: Sit down at a table and eat. No T.V. or mobile phones. Eat your meal and be attentive to how it tastes and feels. Enjoy your meal and note when you start to feel full. Listen to your body and enable yourself to effortlessly quit eating when you feel full and satisfied.

11. Devise a Bedtime Routine

If you're exhausted and not eating adequately you won't have the energy required to concentrate. much of anything. And the sad reality is that most of us don't eat properly or get enough sleep.

Focus on having the same bedtime every night.

You want to cultivate the habit of going to sleep on time and listening to your body by being more conscious and focused on how you feel and when you are weary.

That way you give your body what it needs - which is good rest.

Most of us ignore when our body is sleepy, staying online longer, watching just one more Netflix program, or playing games on our phone when we should be heading to bed.

So concentrate on the structure of your nights so that you naturally go to bed when your body is telling you that it needs rest. Not anytime you "feel tired".

Action Item: Plan out your evening and establish a bedtime. Notice how you feel during the evening and retire to bed when your body sends you indications that it is exhausted.

12. Make a Game of Clearing Up Clutter

Clear out your workplace, your vehicle, and your room so that you feel quiet, tranquil, and serene.

One fun approach that we clear up clutter with our kids is to set a timer for only 5 minutes and create a game out of it. Whoever puts away the most items wins!

Get in the habit of cleaning out your workplace desk at the end of the day. Get in the habit of tidying up the kitchen before you go to bed. Get in the habit of cleaning up your email.

You don't want any extra distractions to sap your concentration. Plus the sheer act of concentrating on these modest organized activities every day helps to rebuild that old attention "muscle".

Action Item: Look around the area around you and over the next 3 minutes, start cleaning up objects that can be placed away someplace out of sight or tucked away (trash can, bookshelf, etc.)

13. Reward Yourself

Make a game out of accomplishing your everyday routine. Humans are driven by incentives and penalties, so make sure that you set up a reward for finishing your duties. You want to develop positive connections around attaining your objectives.

You will channel these emotions of achievement into concentrating on your broader objectives, so it's crucial to reward yourself for keeping on target.

Another suggestion for boosting attention that I've learned is that when you do become distracted don't accomplish things on your to-do list, or don't fulfill a promise that you've given yourself, there has to be a consequence.

Consequences for failing your concentration tasks are highly essential because when you don't do something that you know you should, you experience a small amount of guilt and if that regret is allowed to grow it will drain your sentiments of optimism and drive. A guilty conscience is counter-productive.

I'm not proposing to "punish" you. But I am saying there needs to be a consequence so that you feel like you've "atoned" for messing up.

One fantastic "consequence" that you may have for yourself is to give to a cause that you believe in. That way you still feel good about yourself and can channel those positive sentiments towards your objectives again; this will help you retain your concentration.

Action Item: When you are preparing your to-do list, also set out prizes for getting things done, and a low-risk penalty if you don't finish anything. If you need inspiration, try out these methods to treat yourself.

14. Focus on Your Posture

The third approach to enhance concentration is to pay attention to your own body.

Focus on your posture while you're standing. When you're sitting in the automobile. When you're walking. Etc.

Focus on making sure your spine is straight. Make sure your shoulders are back. Your head should be erect.

Good posture is vital. It helps you be healthy. It makes you more efficient. Focusing on your posture also provides you with a tool to assist you enhance your attention.

Action Item: Right now, while you're reading this article, straighten your back, bring your shoulders back, and maintain your head erect. Notice how amazing it feels and practice this throughout the day.

Final Thoughts on Ways to Improve Focus

Focusing better can allow you to be more productive, successful, and all-around happier.

There are various strategies to boost attention, such as developing a to-do list, setting focus blocks, thinking about your objectives, and more.

Bit by bit you may train your "focus muscle" to be stronger, and you can do everything you set your mind to.

If you want additional strategies for concentrating on your objectives and avoiding distractions then

Setting Up Your Focus Environment

Maintaining attention in the office may be a difficulty. Colleagues conversing, movements in the corner of the eye, scraping sounds from furniture, buzzing fans, insufficient ventilation, glaring sunshine, or visual distractions such as brilliant colors, patterns, and crowded bookcases. It is crucial to eliminate negative distractions in the work environment as it has a direct influence on well-being, efficiency, and productivity. In this post, we discuss several practical ways to eliminate distractions and establish a healthy and pleasant work environment.

1. **Create a balanced sound environment**

    You obtain the ideal circumstances for a decent sound environment if you concentrate on room acoustics early in the design phase. It always pays off to equip the premises from the outset with acoustic ceilings and sound-dampening floor covering. With the aid of interior design, you then reinforce a healthy sound environment, via upholstered furniture, sound absorbers, curtains, plants, carpets, sound-absorbing tabletops, and furniture with wheels. Good acoustics in the workplace is not about producing a fully quiet working environment, but rather about balancing the sound and establishing optimal sound settings for many sorts of activity.

Read more about acoustics and how you create conditions for a pleasant sound environment

2. Define zones with varied degrees of concentration

When arranging your work environment, it is crucial to think about how various settings are located about each other. locations for work demanding focus, for example, need to be segregated from locations where there is a lot of movement and contact between individuals. A good start is thus to split the workplace into several zones, for example, an active zone where there is pulse and movement, a zone for semi-attention where you may work focused but with some crosstalk, and a zone for high focus where you work undisturbed without chatting. This sets the circumstances for everyone to do their jobs throughout the day in the best possible manner.

3. Minimize visual impressions

A dirty or untidy workplace with a lot of impressions, motions, information, and vivid colors implies that we deliberately or unintentionally continually have something distracting in the corner of our eyes. A more regulated and serene work environment, where impressions are cleansed, gives better circumstances for our brain to concentrate on the present task and produces work serenity. In interior design, you might consider that closed or partly closed storage offers a calmer image than, for example, open shelves crowded with objects. With the aid of ceiling-hung or floor-standing screens, soft sitting furniture with high backs, or storage solutions, you may separate the work area so that the eye does not look as far into the room. Another example is placing frosted film over areas of window panes where there is a lot of activity outside, then you limit distractions but still allow positive sunshine to pass through.

4. Choose an earthy color palette

Colors that are near nature's color range, such as green and earthy tones, have a specific influence on people's capacity to recuperate and are consequently chosen in most workplaces. Earthy and subdued hues that go tone on tone give a tranquil mood and are also simple to blend while retaining the uniform and harmonious image. Avoid patterns on huge surfaces, strong hues, or too many distinct colors in the same place.

5. Encourage movement

An unpleasant working posture may be a negative distraction in itself. We, humans, are created to move, thus the design of the work area and the interior design itself must facilitate mobility. Choose furniture that is meant to stimulate mobility and create diversity throughout the day by presenting diverse locations to swap between. Your next position is your finest position!

6. Make it possible to regulate the light

The demand for light fluctuates over the day and the year, depending on what work we have in front of us. It also alters over life - elderly individuals typically require different and more light than younger ones. Flexible solutions and the ability to independently manage the light offer numerous benefits, simply because we all have different tastes and demands. This may, for example, imply dimmable luminaires, curtains, blinds, or moveable illumination.

7. Manage digital distractions

Cell phones and laptops may be big distractions if not utilized effectively. To limit digital distractions, you may turn off alerts or use app blockers that prohibit access to social media and other distractions during work hours. You may also use email filtering to prioritize critical messages and turn off immediate alerts.

The human capacity to multitask is a fiction, in reality, our brains can only focus on, and take in, one thing at a time. Our brain only has one processor and as soon as we multitask, the brain needs to transition between multiple tasks. If we are interrupted, it might take up to twenty minutes before we restore the same attention.

Daily Rituals for Improved Attention

We all have habits that help us operate more successfully. These routines may operate as a road map, helping you remain focused and keeping you on track throughout your day. The more time and effort you save, the more productive you will be.

Your working rituals comprise your habits, routine, and schedule. They either enable you to work smarter or inhibit your productivity. By following these eight daily routines, you will empower yourself to be hyper-focused and productive all day long.

1. **Determine your optimal wake-up time and bedtime.**

There is no miraculous one-size-fits-all timetable that will suit everyone. Some of us are early risers who like the morning hours. Others of us are night owls who discover our creativity fires after the rest of the world has gone to sleep.

Most of us have a fixed wake-up hour based on our commitments and duties, the demands of our families, and employment requirements. In general, most of us require roughly eight hours of sleep to perform at our best. Your sleep schedule should take all of this into consideration.

Set a bedtime that you can regularly stick to on both workday and weekend evenings. This will set a timetable for your body's internal clock, so your body understands when to sleep and when to wake. This will increase the quality of your sleep so that you continuously feel refreshed and ready to operate at your best.

2. Get going.

An excellent method to break the veil of grogginess you experience when you first wake up is simply exercising your body. Likewise, after being pent-up sitting at your desk all day, stepping out for an afternoon walk or some exercise might help clear your thoughts.

Whether it entails yoga stretches, hitting the treadmill, or going for a stroll, getting up and moving about is a terrific method to help your mind concentrate. Several studies have discovered that the areas of the brain that govern thinking and memory are bigger and better developed in those who exercise frequently than in those who don't.

Research demonstrates that when we exercise, blood pressure and blood flow rise everywhere in the body. More blood provides more energy and oxygen, which are crucial to helping our brains operate better. Ensure your daily routine involves activity to keep your mind and your body working effectively.

3. Launch yourself into your day.

Popular motivational speaker and author Brian Tracy recommends individuals eat their largest frog first thing in the morning -- meaning that if you start your day with your biggest, most essential, or most feared chore, the rest of your day will be simple by comparison. This might be a terrific approach to start yourself moving on a challenging assignment that is hanging over your head.

Unless, of course, the fear of beginning your day with a gigantic assignment backfires and makes it much more difficult to stay focused and start working. If that's the case, start your morning by taking on something essential but relatively simple to do.

The objective is to discover a means to propel oneself into a productive attitude. If crossing off a few items on your daily to-do list gets you moving, then do that! If you adore taking on that huge, monstrous assignment first thing so you can get it over with, then, by all means, go at it!

4. Use self-orienting questions to retain your concentration.

Throughout the day, if you feel your focus slide or find yourself completing unnecessary or irrelevant things to fill time, ask yourself the following questions:

- What's the most essential thing I could be doing right now?
- How can I get this done quicker and more efficiently?

- What's a better approach to do this task?

These simple yet effective questions may be used to help you restore your concentration and maintain your attention where it needs to be. Are you doing what you need to be doing? If not, what should you be doing? The objective of this is to be more mindful of how you're spending your time and not simply letting minutes drift by. If you're taking a break, that's OK, but make sure you have specified how long your breather is, and know what job you want to perform when you go back to work.

5. Do it immediately.

The only way to get something done is to do it. It truly is that easy, yet we frequently put things off because we're caught up in doing something else, or we're focused on some future goal. But if there is anything that has to be done immediately, simply do it!

Often, tiny things may crop up, but we put them off since we're doing something else. If the tiny job can be done pretty quickly, then don't put it off -- just do it right then.

This minimizes procrastination and protects your to-do list from ballooning out of hand with minor jobs that will soon consume your entire day. By knocking off these tiny duties when they pop up, you'll leave yourself more time to concentrate on the major issues.

6. **Build in brain breaks.**

Our brains are only capable of continually focusing on anything for a specific length of time. By taking small pauses, preferably approximately once an hour, you give your mind time to decompress and rest so it can refocus and concentrate again.

Psychologist Alejandro Lleras observed that participants who were given brief breaks throughout 50-minute assignments did better than those who worked straight through. Lleras observed that minor distractions from a task may greatly boost people's capacity to concentrate on that work for an extended duration.

The research explored a phenomena called "vigilance decrement," or the loss of one's "attentional resources." This might happen when you start doing badly on a subject you're having a hard time concentrating on. That's when you should take a quick mental vacation. This offers your brain time to deactivate, and when you go back to work, your mind is better ready to concentrate.

7. **Reflect on what you've done and how to improve.**

At the end of the day, take a few minutes for self-reflection. Ask yourself some questions that will help you judge how well you did and what you may do better tomorrow. These include:

- What did I achieve today?
- Did I achieve what I set out to, and everything I needed to?
- What did I do well today?
- What errors were made?
- What choices did I make today?
- Why did I make these choices and not other options?
- Were these choices effective?

The idea is to observe how well you're doing and keeping on target. whether you do this regularly, you can measure whether you're making consistent progress toward your objectives and discover what areas you need to concentrate on and enhance.

8. Prepare for tomorrow.

This little habit is certain to help enhance your productivity tomorrow. Take a few minutes at the end of your workday and spell out to yourself what your objectives are for the following day. This is a time to think through the process of how you will achieve what you need to do. Consider these questions:

- What are your main priorities?

- What jobs must you get done?
- What obstacles or concerns could arise?
- What problems could hinder you from keeping focused?

Often, we remain relatively focused until something unexpected crops up. Perhaps you receive a phone call or an email that takes your attention. Perhaps you were drawn into a chat with a co-worker. Think through ways to avoid these problems and be prepared for what's on your plate.

Chapter 7

Taming Technology

In an era of omnipresent technology and digital connectedness, mastering technology is critical for enabling meaningful work, maintaining attention, and maintaining cognitive well-being. This chapter delves into evidence-based tactics and practical ideas for navigating digital distractions, optimizing technology use, and developing mindful engagement with digital tools among the challenges of modern living.

The Effects of Technology on Attention and Productivity

Technology influences both attentional dynamics and cognitive performance.

Digital distractions, such as alerts and social media feeds, can disrupt attention and cognitive concentration.

Technology improves access to information, communication, and productivity tools, enabling cooperation and knowledge exchange.

Understanding Digital Distractions

Digital distractions take different forms, including:

Overload of alerts from email, social media, and messaging platforms can disturb focus and lead to constant partial attention.

Excessive exposure to internet content and stimulation might cause cognitive overload and impede decision-making.

Digital gadgets' seamless task-switching capabilities encourage multitasking, affecting work efficiency and quality.

Strategies for Taming Technology
Optimizing technology use necessitates purposeful practice and the strategic application of digital wellness methods.

Implement Digital Detox periods.

Set set periods for withdrawing from digital gadgets and internet sites. Engage in offline activities to replenish brain resources and improve mental clarity.

Establish Device-Free Zones.

Designate specific areas (e.g., bedroom, dining room) as device-free zones to encourage face-to-face interactions, relaxation, and uninterrupted attention.

Leverage Digital Tools for Productivity

Use productivity applications and digital tools only when necessary to simplify processes, organize activities, and reduce cognitive strain. Use technology to increase productivity while avoiding information overload.

Customize Notification Settings

Disable unnecessary alerts and customize notification settings to reduce disruptions and maintain attentiveness. Prioritize essential alerts and messages to improve work prioritization and time management.

Practice Mindful Technology Use

Setting purposeful limits and practicing present-moment awareness will help you cultivate mindfulness in your digital connections. Mindful technology usage promotes deep work, prolonged attention, and cognitive well-being.

Real-World Applications for Taming Technology

Consider the following real-world examples to demonstrate the practical ramifications of taming technology.

- Entrepreneurs use digital minimalism to reduce workflows and optimize task management, resulting in increased productivity and work-life balance.
- Academic Excellence: A student uses digital detox times during study sessions to reduce distractions and improve knowledge retention during exam preparation.

- Establishing device-free zones at home promotes relaxation, improves interpersonal relationships, and fosters awareness in daily life.

Digital Detox Strategies

In a hyper connected society where digital technologies penetrate all aspects of everyday life, applying digital detox tactics is critical for maintaining mental health, encouraging deep work, and regaining attentional control. This subchapter delves into evidence-based methods and practical strategies for unplugging digital gadgets, reducing digital distractions, and cultivating mindfulness in the digital era.

Understanding Digital Detox

Digital detox is defined as planned periods away from digital devices and online platforms to improve mental clarity, reduce stress, and restore cognitive well-being. Key features of digital detox are:

- Limiting screen time by unplugging from devices like cellphones, PCs, and tablets.
- Offline activities include reading actual books, outdoor activities, and hobbies that don't rely on technology.
- Promoting Mindful Engagement: Using technology to improve productivity and well-being by focusing on the present moment.

The importance of digital detox.

The widespread impact of digital technology on attentional dynamics and cognitive function emphasizes the need for digital detox:

- Disconnecting from digital gadgets reduces tension and anxiety, promoting relaxation.
- Digital detox improves focus and productivity by reducing distractions.
- Improved Sleep Quality: Limiting screen time before bedtime improves peaceful sleep and reduces interruptions caused by excessive technology usage.

Evidence-based Digital Detox Strategies

Implementing digital detox tactics needs purposeful practice and careful application of evidence-based techniques:

Establishing Digital-Free Zones

Designate particular spaces (such as the bedroom or dining room) as digital-free zones to encourage face-to-face conversations, relaxation, and uninterrupted attention.

Create a distinct reading nook or hobby area in your house where digital gadgets are not permitted, creating an environment favorable to offline activity and relaxation.

Set Screen Time Limits

Set daily or weekly screen time limitations for digital devices and internet platforms. Screen time may be successfully monitored and managed via parental control settings or mobile applications.

For example, use smartphone applications that measure screen time and provide use statistics to discover trends of excessive screen time and modify accordingly.

Implementing Technology-Free Hours

Set aside specified time intervals (e.g., evenings, and weekends) to unplug from digital gadgets and engage in offline activities. Use this time to relax, reconnect with loved ones, and pursue hobbies free of internet distractions.

Schedule a "tech-free hour" before bedtime to unwind and prepare for a good night's sleep. Engage in soothing activities like reading a book or practicing meditation.

Participating in nature walks and outdoor activities.

Disconnect from digital gadgets and reconnect with nature by going on nature walks, doing outdoor activities, and exercising. Immersion in nature improves mindfulness and stress reduction.

Take regular nature walks in local parks or nature reserves, leaving digital gadgets at home or in a backpack, to reap the therapeutic advantages of outdoor activities.

Practice Mindful Technology Use

Setting purposeful limits and practicing present-moment awareness will help you cultivate mindfulness in your digital connections. Mindful technology usage promotes deep work, prolonged attention, and cognitive well-being.

For example, before using digital gadgets, take a minute to pause and reflect on your objectives. Consider why you are using the gadget and whether it is consistent with your beliefs and priorities.

Real-world Applications of Digital Detox

The following real-world instances demonstrate the practical ramifications of digital detox strategies:

Entrepreneurs use digital detox approaches to preserve work-life balance and minimize burnout, resulting in increased productivity and well-being.

A parent sets tech-free hours for family dinners to foster meaningful talks and enhance relationships.

Why Regular digital detox weekends promote mental and emotional well-being, emphasizing self-care and mindfulness.

Using technology carefully

With these methods for utilizing technology with mindfulness, you may avoid continual distractions from your gadgets and focus on what is important.

By being present and mindful in your use of technology, you may say goodbye to stress and welcome to enhanced attention and mood overall. Furthermore, being conscious can help to avoid some of the more unpleasant side effects of excessive technology usage, such as headaches, eye strain, and poor sleep.

Being careful of how you use technology may even enhance your connections with others by reducing distractions from your devices. So, take a deep breath and learn about some methods for using technology more consciously. Your mind and body will thank you for this!

How Conscious Are You About Your Technology?

You may not realize how "mindless" you are when utilizing technology. As a result, it may be beneficial to begin with a brief self-assessment.

Mindfulteachers.org provides a useful, brief quiz that will provide you with some insight into the nature of your thinking regarding your usage of technology. By answering a series of true/false questions, you may quickly determine if your relationship with technology is healthy or requires care.

Here are some thought-provoking questions:

- Did you check your phone instead of engaging with the person in front of you?
- Have others expressed concern about your excessive phone use?
- Have you ever felt lonely looking at images from an event you weren't invited to?

If you replied "true" to these questions, you may want to reconsider how you utilize technology.

Be mindful of posture when sitting at your desk.

Mindfulness is all about being present in the moment and mindful of changing sensations in the body and mind. And because you may spend a significant amount of time sitting at a desk, this presents an excellent chance to practice mindfulness.

For example, how do you sit right now? Are you slouched or sitting upright? Set the purpose to sit in good posture: maintain your back straight but not stiff, engage your core, and use your ergonomic setup as intended.

Then, look at additional ways to maintain a healthy posture, including altering your chair and replacing your display.

Use Technology Purposefully.

We've all seen what happens when people use technology without thinking. Consider someone who is so engrossed in their smartphone that they walk headlong into a streetlamp or someone who is on a date but checks texts throughout the talk.

On the other hand, utilizing technology deliberately entails using it in a way that is consistent with your aims and ideals. This appears to be completely different and can be a freeing experience.

Consider how you use social media. Instead of passively scanning countless feeds, utilize it just to communicate with friends and family. Similarly, you may utilize technology wisely to achieve specific health and fitness goals. Most smart devices have activity-tracking applications, and there are several third-party apps to help you keep active.

You may also refer to this list of techniques to prevent becoming a smartphone addict. Consider utilizing one piece of technology at a time, having a designated space in your house where you keep and use your smartphone, and removing all electronics from the bedroom, where your primary emphasis should be on sleeping.

Be aware of how technology affects you when you use it.

The science is clear: social media makes you depressed. By paying greater attention to your current experience on

Facebook or Instagram, you may notice varied degrees of FOMO, desire, envy, or jealousy. Recognizing that you are experiencing these sensations is a vital first step toward taking action.

After all, our mental experiences are the same as our life experiences. So, you want to engage in activities that encourage pleasant mental experiences while avoiding those that make you feel inadequate or discontent with yourself.

In addition to tracking your emotions in real-time, experiment with monitoring your breath while using technology such as social media. You may realize that you are holding your breath or increasing your breathing rate when exploring social media or reading the news online. By taking calm, deep breaths, you may be able to mitigate the harmful effects of technology on your well-being.

If you practice meditation regularly and have established a decent level of focus, paying attention to how you feel while using technology will become simpler. If you don't already, download one of the many meditation apps and start practicing now.

For example, the Waking Up app provides guided meditations and teacher chats, as well as "mindful moments" to help you achieve equanimity throughout the day.

Set boundaries and create a schedule.

Because technology is frequently designed to catch our attention, scheduling can be an effective approach to mitigate the negative effects of screen time.

Experiment with setting up certain times when you use technology. For example, you may set aside 30 minutes on Saturday morning to check LinkedIn for new alerts, and 15 minutes each morning, afternoon, and evening to send text messages. Alternatively, you may set a timer to turn off your Wi-Fi at a specific time each night.

You may also employ schedules to help you be more aware. 30 minutes of practice each morning may have a life-changing effect on your mood, anxiety levels, and compassion for others.

Be mindful of online interactions.

Do you communicate with people online in the same manner as you would face-to-face? According to some of the comments left on social media, many individuals are unaware of how angry or harsh they can be.

As a result, while communicating with others online, try to be aware of how you come across. You may achieve this by envisioning yourself speaking to someone face to face.

If you wish to improve your mindful communication skills, try the following Buddhist advice: only talk or say things that are kind, beneficial, and true. If what you have to say does not include all three of these adjectives, do not speak it.

Limit unnecessary non-human notifications.

Apps, internet services, corporations, and influencers demand your attention. They attempt to capture your attention with a slew of badges, notification bars, noises, emails, and text messages.

Constant distractions and attention-grabbing alerts are detrimental to attentive technology use. Fortunately, there are various strategies to reduce notification fatigue and increase your chances of avoiding these distractions, such as turning off all unneeded, non-human notifications.

Using Technology Mindfully to Feel Peace.

Mindfulness may help you utilize technology to your advantage rather than against you. You may significantly increase your well-being by engaging and purposefully using technology. You'll be more fascinating to others around you, have more time for the important things, and feel better about yourself as a person.

Chapter 8

Managing Distractions from Relationships

There are several impediments to truly connecting with others. In today's environment, technology and activity rob our ability to be present and communicate with others around us.

We all want strong connections with others, but if we are to break down the boundaries that keep us from expressing our genuine selves, we must first recognize the source of the problem. We need to treat the disease, not just the symptoms.

Fear hinders genuine relationships.

Fear is one of the most prevalent fundamental causes of social isolation. We are afraid of rejection, failure, and being judged. We are afraid of the unpleasantness of unfamiliar settings or of failing to meet expectations.

One of our most fundamental desires is to be recognized and liked. Unfortunately, our concerns may paralyze us, leaving us unable or unable to take the risks required to discover the authentic relationships we seek.

We have a strong yearning for connection because God made us to need both others and Him. We are afraid to open up because we live in a world full of broken relationships that do not represent what God intended for us.

We need to stop hiding.

According to the Bible's account of the earliest human beings, they began in a perfect connection with God. They finally ended the relationship by believing falsehoods about Him and betraying Him. When they realized what they'd done, dread gripped them, and their reaction was to physically hide from God so He wouldn't see their faults.

We are still hiding from God and one another. Anyone can see that our society is full of broken relationships and that it is simple to put on a mask and hide from God.

Only when we conquer our worries and stop concealing can we experience the delight of a closer relationship with God and others?

The good news is that we are not condemned to isolation. Jesus overcame our brokenness and made it possible for us to have a relationship with God again. God gives every one of us a connection with Himself, but we must all decide if we are willing to stop hiding and embrace it.

Only when we conquer our worries and stop concealing can we experience the delight of a closer relationship with God and others?

Building Bridges to Community: Intentional Relationships

Many of us have never considered the possibility that there is something deeper underneath the surface distractions of life that restrict us from connecting with people. So, how can we recognize the anxieties that drive our excessive use of technology and the attraction of busyness?

The following are some things to consider as you work to develop deeper relationships and prevent isolation.

Next steps:

- Fear of losing out: How much time do you spend using technology during the day? Is your time spent on social media stopping you from developing relationships with "real" people? Find perspective and seek assistance in dealing with the allure of social media.
- Fear of rejection: Do you wait for someone to approach you? Are you terrified of what others would say if you sought out? You provide value to relationships and have a lot to give people. Take a chance and contact someone you want to spend time with. Consider joining a local group to meet new people, or locate a Cru community. Learn more about where your genuine worth originates from.
- Fear of failure: Do you have a busy schedule that prevents you from socializing? Are you so terrified of losing a ball that you forego opportunities to interact with those who are most important to you? Learn how to intentionally make extra space in your life.
- Fear of judgment: Do you hide aspects of yourself from others in your relationships? Are you concerned that others would not accept you for who

you truly are? Relationships gain depth when we are vulnerable with one another. Take a step towards a trusted friend and reveal a part of yourself that deserves to be known. Read more about being open to God and others

Understanding Relationship Dynamics and Focus.

Relationships of all types are an essential component of being human. They are locations where we may meet our basic requirements while also feeling connected to the people around us.

However, there are times when the people closest to us annoy us greatly in their attempts to meet our basic needs. There is a dynamic at work that we cannot perceive. Why do we continue to connect with someone who repeatedly upsets us? Why don't certain individuals meet our needs in relationships? As we go on to the drama triangle, I'll address these questions below. The drama triangle is an effective tool for understanding the underlying dynamics of relationships. With this information, you should be able to identify your position in the drama triangle and break free from it, allowing you to have healthy relationships and meet your needs.

1. The Drama Triangle

The Drama Triangle is a concept coined by psychologist Stephen Karpman that outlines a prevalent pattern in dysfunctional interpersonal interactions. It depicts three unique roles that humans typically play in dramatic situations: victim, persecutor, and rescuer. These roles are not set; individuals can swap between them depending on the situation. We shall look at these responsibilities below:

- The Victim:

Victims feel powerless and oppressed, and they blame others for their troubles. They frequently want compassion, support, and rescue from others. They may use guilt or deception to get attention and keep others interested in their difficulties.

- The Persecutor

The Persecutor assumes an aggressive or domineering position. They criticize, accuse, or attack others, frequently feeling superior or justified in their actions. They may use intimidation or coercion to retain power over others.

- The Rescuer:

The Rescuer attempts to save or heal the Victim. They provide unsolicited advice, assistance, or solutions, feeling they are responsible for resolving other people's issues. Rescuers frequently have a need to be needed, which might foster the Victim's reliance. The persecutor and victim engage, as do the rescuer and victim; however, the persecutor and rescuer do not interact because everyone is striving for the role of victim. Fear is important to all of the roles. Persecutors dread losing control, while rescuers fear losing their cause. Rescuers rely on victims to boost their self-esteem because it offers them a false sense of superiority, which is fundamentally a feeling of inadequacy. Rescuers create dependency by being necessary to those who play the victim.

Ego state and transactional analysis

If you discover that you play any of the roles in your life, treat yourself with care and empathy. Do not blame yourself, as they are mostly unconscious ways of negotiating relationships.

To better clarify the drama triangle, we'll look at the ego states that arise when it occurs. Ego states are an important term in transactional analysis (TA), a psychological theory created by Eric Berne. According to TA, people have three distinct ego states: parent, adult, and child. These ego states indicate various patterns of thought, mood, and behavior that we exhibit throughout interactions with others.

The Parent ego state represents the internalized voice of authoritative persons from our history, such as parents or other carers. It is composed of two aspects:

a.   Nurturing Parent: This facet highlights the good and loving behaviors acquired from nurturing figures. It can provide support, comfort, and protection.

b.   Critical Parent: This characteristic shows negative and critical behaviors taught by authoritative persons. It may be judgemental, controlling, or demanding.

The Drama Triangle, which explains three roles that individuals perform in dysfunctional or harmful interactions, might help us better understand the Parent ego state:

- Persecutor: The Critical Parent is frequently related to the position of Persecutor. This position requires accusing, condemning, and punishing people. The Persecutor may take a superior or aggressive stance.

- Rescuer: The Nurturing Parent can take on the role of a rescuer. This job is attempting to assist or preserve others, frequently disregarding their autonomy or needs. Rescuers may exhibit overprotective or supportive behavior.

2.   Adult Ego State:

The Adult ego state represents logical thought, objective observation, and problem-solving. It entails assessing data, making informed decisions, and engaging with people maturely and responsibly. The Adult ego state is emotionally neutral and focuses on the current world.

In the Drama Triangle, the Adult ego state is considered a healthier alternative to the Parent roles. The Adult avoids accusing or rescuing actions and instead seeks constructive solutions and clear communication.

3.   Child's Ego State:

The Child's ego state represents the emotions, feelings, and actions we have carried over from our childhood experiences.

In the Drama Triangle, the Child's ego state might appear in the following roles:

• Victim: The Adapted Child may occasionally play the role of the Victim, feeling powerless, oppressed, or victimized. This character may seek compassion or support from others despite feeling helpless to change the circumstances.

• Persecutor: When uncontrolled, the Free Child might take on the role of the Persecutor by acting out, rebelling, or participating in harmful activity. This position may result in lash outs against others or violations of social standards. It's vital to remember that the Drama Triangle portrays unhealthy and dysfunctional patterns of interaction. The objective is to transition to more constructive ego states, such as adults, which promote successful communication, problem resolution, and healthier relationships.

a.   Adapted Child: This characteristic displays learned actions and attitudes shaped by cultural norms and expectations. It may include cooperation, conformity, and repressing one's wants to fulfill external obligations.

b.   The Free Child component shows our personality's spontaneity, creativity, and delight. It entails expressing emotions, demonstrating interest, and participating in creative or imaginative activities.

Understanding the Drama Triangle

Here's how they can be linked: a person operating from a Parent ego state can play either the Persecutor or the Rescuer role, depending on whether they're being critical or loving. A person operating from a Child ego state, particularly the Adapted Child state, is more likely to take on the Victim position in the drama triangle. The Adult ego state is capable of guiding an individual out of the drama triangle by objectively assessing the circumstance and exhibiting problem-solving actions.

In the drama triangle, we may feel helpless, scared, and disappointed because our needs are not being addressed. It might be a dynamic that we have grown up with and that seems familiar to us, making it difficult to let go of since it is a dysfunctional method of attempting to meet your needs that does not work and causes additional worry, frustration, and helplessness.

Reflection

Below are some thoughtful questions to ask yourself, and I highly recommend writing them down in a diary and sitting with them. Be nice to yourself, but be honest.

- How do you tell whether you're in the drama triangle?
- What is your experience, and how does it feel?
- How do you act when you are in the Victim role?
- How do you act as the Persecutor?
- What do you do in the Rescuer role?
- Which ego state do you see yourself slipping into when playing each character in the drama triangle?

The Empowerment Dynamic (TED

David Emerald invented The Empowerment Dynamic (TED), which is an alternative to the Drama Triangle. It focuses on building good and powerful connections via three main roles: Creator, Challenger, and Coach. These jobs promote personal responsibility, accountability, and development.

1. The creator:

The Creator bears responsibility for their life and surroundings. They understand that they can determine their answers and behaviors. Instead of playing the victim, they become proactive, focusing on finding solutions and attaining their objectives.

Use the creator role by:

- Creating clear objectives and describing what you want to accomplish.

- Accepting responsibility for your decisions, actions, and consequences.

- Maintaining a good attitude and concentrating on possibilities and chances.

- Pursuing personal development and viewing setbacks as chances to learn.

2. The challenger:

The Challenger serves as a supporting catalyst for development and change. Rather than being a Persecutor, they offer constructive comments, challenge limiting beliefs, and promote personal growth.

Use the challenger role by:

- Giving honest and constructive comments to others while remaining respectful and compassionate.

- Encouraging people to challenge their assumptions and beliefs.

- Pushing yourself to leave your comfort zone and accept new experiences.

- Assisting others with their personal development by providing direction and encouragement.

3. The Coach:

The Coach provides help, direction, and encouragement to others. Unlike the Rescuer, they allow people to find their answers and make their own choices.

Use the Coach role to:

• Active listening and open-ended inquiries can assist others in achieving clarity and insights.

• Supporting and encouraging individuals while enabling them to take control of

• Their acts.

• Assisting others in identifying their talents and resources for overcoming obstacles.

• Promoting self-reflection and personal growth in others.

Applying the Empowerment Dynamic

By embracing the Empowerment Dynamic, you transition from a victim perspective to one of personal action and progress. You take responsibility for your life, help others improve, and create a collaborative and empowering atmosphere. Playing the roles of Creator, Challenger, and Coach can result in more satisfying relationships and personal development.

Remember that continuously embodying these roles requires time and practice. Be gentle with yourself and others while you make this transition. Consider obtaining advice from a coach, mentor, or counselor who can help you develop these powerful abilities.

Reflection

Again, consider these questions as a method to work towards improving how you connect with others in your life. Be nice to yourself, but be honest.

- Which TED position appeals to you the most: creator, coach, or challenger?
- Which of the TED responsibilities do you find the most challenging?
- What could you do to transition from Victim to Creator?
- What could you do to change from Persecutor to Challenger?
- What could you do to transition from the Rescuer to the Coach role?
- Who in your life, or history, are inspiring examples of Creators?
- What about them inspires you and makes you want to be like them?

In the linked world formed by digital technology, interpersonal dynamics have a significant impact on attentional concentration, cognitive function, and general well-being. This subchapter delves into the complexities of relationship dynamics, explaining their influence on attentional focus and providing evidence-based practices for promoting cognitive clarity during social interactions.

The Effect of Relationships on Attentional Focus

Relationships, whether personal or professional, have a substantial influence on attention and cognitive processes.

- Social Engagement: Relationships with family, friends, and coworkers impact attention and mood management.

- Emotional Contagion: Interpersonal emotions can impact cognitive function and attentiveness.

- Effective communication increases attentional involvement, whereas misunderstanding or disagreements can lead to fragmentation. Relationships and Attentional Focus different sorts of connections (e.g., personal, family, professional) affect attentional focus in distinct ways:

- Romantic relationships and close friendships affect attentional states through emotional connection and support.

- Family dynamics influence attentional processes and cognitive responses during interpersonal encounters.

- Colleagues and professional networks impact attentional involvement in work-related situations.

Strategies to Maintain Cognitive Clarity in Relationships

To maintain attentional concentration and cognitive clarity, it is necessary to navigate interpersonal dynamics through purposeful practices and strategic methods.

Establishing Boundaries

Set clear limits in relationships to prioritize cognitive involvement while minimizing distractions. Communicate clearly about your attentional demands and preferences.

Negotiate dedicated "focus time" with romantic partners or family members to reduce distractions and encourage intense work during specific times.

Practice Active Listening

Engage in active listening during interpersonal encounters to improve attention and mutual comprehension. To promote good communication, validate and reflect on other people's opinions.

For example, during talks with coworkers or acquaintances, use reflective listening skills (e.g., paraphrasing, summarising) to retain attention and increase cognitive clarity.

Developing Empathy and Emotional Regulation

Develop empathy and emotional management abilities so that you may effectively negotiate interpersonal dynamics. Recognize and control emotional reactions to increase cognitive resilience and interpersonal harmony.

Empathy-building techniques, such as perspective-taking and compassion meditation, can help to improve emotional intelligence and mutual understanding in relationships.

Prioritize quality interactions.

Prioritize quality over quantity in your relationships by engaging in meaningful encounters that foster attentional engagement and emotional connection.

Schedule frequent "tech-free" trips with friends or family members to develop face-to-face conversations and strengthen emotional relationships in the absence of digital distractions.

Practice Mindful Communication

Cultivate mindful communication methods to improve attentional concentration and cognitive clarity during interpersonal encounters. Pause and ponder before reacting to improve communication effectiveness.

For example, use mindfulness practices (such as deep breathing and body awareness) during talks to regulate attention and improve present-moment awareness.

Real-world applications of relationship dynamics and focus.

Consider the following real-world examples to demonstrate how relationship dynamics affect attentional focus:

- In romantic relationships, couples use active listening and empathy to improve communication and retain cognitive clarity.
- Siblings create limits and prioritize quality interactions to improve family dynamics and emotional resilience.
- Professional Networks: Colleagues practice mindful communication to improve engagement and collaboration in working encounters.

Communicating boundaries with partners.

Setting clear and respectful boundaries with love partners is critical for developing healthy, rewarding relationships and retaining cognitive clarity throughout interpersonal interactions. This subchapter digs into the complexities of boundary-setting in intimate relationships, providing evidence-based solutions and practical advice for effective communication and mutual understanding.

The significance of boundaries in romantic relationships.

Boundaries define individual needs, preferences, and boundaries in romantic relationships, influencing communication dynamics and emotional closeness.

- Boundaries support personal autonomy and self-expression in relationships.

- Clear boundaries promote emotional well-being and reduce interpersonal conflict.

- Effective boundary setting promotes open, honest communication and mutual respect among partners.

Types of Boundaries in Romantic Relationships

Different sorts of boundaries have diverse roles in romantic relationships:

- Physical boundaries include guidelines for contact, personal space, and intimacy.
- Emotional boundaries refer to the parameters of emotional availability, empathy, and support in the relationship.

Establish boundaries for personal time, interests, and shared activities.

Strategies for Effective Communication of Boundaries

Boundary setting involves active communication and sympathetic understanding to foster mutual respect and emotional well-being:

Self-reflection and Clarity

Before starting boundary-setting talks, clarify your personal beliefs, needs, and boundaries. Determine which areas of sensitivity or discomfort necessitate open conversation with your spouse.

Consider your emotional triggers and communication preferences when establishing boundaries around sensitive issues (such as personal space and privacy).

Open and Honest Communication

Have open, honest talks with your spouse about individual limits and relationship expectations. Use "I" phrases to convey wants and feelings without assigning blame or criticism.

Say, for instance, "I value my personal space and would appreciate it if we could discuss plans before making commitments that involve both of us."

Establishing Mutual Agreement.

Negotiate and develop mutual agreements on limits to guarantee shared understanding and respect. Establish relationship standards that respect individual autonomy and emotional well-being.

For example, agree on "alone time" for personal hobbies or self-care activities to respect each other's desire for independence and recharge.

Consistent Reinforcement

Consistently establish limits with forceful conversation and polite behavior. To maintain relationship integrity and emotional safety, respond to boundary infractions swiftly and assertively.

For example, gently remind your spouse to set limits when needed to reinforce mutual respect and emotional awareness in the relationship.

Seeking Professional Support.

Seek couples counseling or relationship therapy to effectively manage boundary issues and communication challenges. Engage in therapeutic interventions to improve emotional intimacy and foster healthy relationship dynamics.

Real-World Examples of Boundary Communication in Relationships

Consider the real-world scenarios below to demonstrate the practical implications of boundary communication in romantic relationships:

- Intimacy Boundaries: Couples discuss personal preferences and boundaries for physical intimacy to improve comfort and emotional connection.
- Establishing time management limits can help partners achieve work-life balance and prioritize quality time together.
- Emotional Support Boundaries: Communicating emotional needs and expectations promotes empathy and understanding within relationships.

Chapter 9

Managing External Distractions

External distractions abound in today's fast-paced and networked society, reducing attentional concentration and productivity. This chapter delves into evidence-based tactics and practical recommendations for efficiently controlling external distractions, promoting deep work, and improving cognitive clarity despite the complications of modern living.

Understanding External Distractions.

External distractions include environmental cues and other elements that divert attention and disturb cognitive processes:

- Digital distractions include notifications, emails, social media, and other digital stimuli that compete for attention and cognitive resources.
- Noise, clutter, and disruptions in the physical environment can disrupt focus and work performance.

- Social interactions, such as unplanned talks and interruptions from coworkers or family members, can disturb workflow and concentration.

The Effect of External Distractions on Cognitive Performance

External distractions have significant effects on cognitive performance and productivity:

- Attention Fragmentation: Diverse attention and task switching hinder efficiency and cognitive engagement.
- Interruptions and diversions reduce productivity and impair goal accomplishment.
- Persistent distractions might lead to tension, worry, and weariness.

Strategies to Manage External Distractions

Optimizing attentional concentration necessitates careful practice and smart application of distraction control strategies.

Designing Distraction-Free Zones

Create specific workstations or distraction-free locations that encourage serious concentration and sustained focus.

Set up a quiet home office with little visual clutter and noise to improve focus and reduce external distractions.

Implementing Time Blocking Techniques.

Set up defined time blocks for concentrated work and attention, limiting interruptions and distractions during allocated intervals.

To increase productivity and preserve attentional concentration, arrange work sessions into concentrated intervals followed by brief breaks using time-blocking strategies (e.g., the Pomodoro Technique).

Managing Digital Notifications

To reduce interruptions and save cognitive resources, turn off unnecessary notifications and prioritize crucial alerts.

Customise notification settings on digital devices to get important updates (e.g., urgent emails, calendar reminders) while turning off non-essential notifications (e.g., social media and app notifications).

Establishing Communication Protocols

Communicate precise communication guidelines to coworkers, family members, and peers to reduce unplanned interruptions and build respect for dedicated work time.

Set clear expectations with coworkers about their availability for meetings and collaborative projects, and designate particular periods for undisturbed work and communication.

Practicing mindfulness and attention training

Develop mindfulness and attentional abilities through meditation, deep breathing exercises, and cognitive training to improve focus and resilience to external distractions.

For example, practice mindfulness techniques (such as mindful breathing and body scan meditation) to improve present-moment awareness and attentional regulation in the face of external stimuli.

Real-World Examples of Managing External Distractions

Consider the real-world situations below to demonstrate the practical consequences of minimizing external distractions:

Workplace Productivity: Employees use distraction management strategies to optimize workflow and decrease interruptions, leading to increased productivity and task completion.

- Establishing limits and communication procedures with family members may reduce distractions during work-from-home arrangements, boosting balance and focus.
- Academic Excellence: Students use distraction management tactics to improve material retention and exam preparation.

Optimizing Workspace for Focus

Creating an optimized workplace is critical for reducing external distractions, encouraging intense focus, and increasing cognitive clarity. This subchapter delves into evidence-based tactics and practical recommendations for planning and organizing a workplace that encourages concentration, productivity, and general well-being in the face of external stimuli and distractions.

Importance of Workspace Optimization

An optimized workspace plays an important role in influencing attentional dynamics and cognitive function.

- A well-designed workstation reduces visual and aural distractions, promoting prolonged focus and concentration.
- Organized workspaces improve productivity by optimizing task completion and goal accomplishment.
- Improves Psychological Well-Being: A visually pleasing and ergonomic workstation promotes emotional comfort and minimizes stress during work hours.

Designing the Ideal Workspace

Optimizing your workstation entails careful design and strategic use of ergonomic and psychological factors.

Ergonomic Considerations

Prioritise ergonomic design aspects to promote physical comfort and prevent musculoskeletal strain.

- Use ergonomic seats and height-adjustable workstations to maintain appropriate posture and reduce pain during long work sessions.
- Optimal lighting: Combine natural light with task lighting to decrease eye strain and improve visual clarity.
- Optimize workflow and reduce physical exertion with an organized workspace.

Minimizing Visual Clutter

- Decluttering and organizing office surfaces can help reduce visual distractions.
- Create a focus-friendly workplace by using relaxing color palettes and simple furnishings.
- Use organizational systems like shelves, file cabinets, and drawer organizers to keep workspaces clutter-free and encourage cognitive orderliness.
- Minimize visual distractions by organizing digital files into folders and decluttering desktops.
- Personalization and Inspiration

- Add personal touches and inspiring aspects to promote emotional connection and motivation:

- Display personal items such as photographs, plants, or mementos to promote happy feelings and well-being.
- Incorporate encouraging quotations or artwork to boost creativity and resilience throughout work sessions.
- Incorporate indoor plants or nature-inspired designs to aid relaxation and cognitive repair throughout professional activities.

Implementing Noise Management Strategies

Reduce auditory distractions and improve acoustic comfort in the workplace environment:

- Use acoustic panels or noise-cancelling headphones to reduce external noise and improve focus.
- Use background music or white noise to reduce distractions and improve attention.

Real-world Applications of Workspace Optimisation

Consider the real-world situations below to demonstrate the practical consequences of workspace optimization:

- Establishing a home office with ergonomic furniture and personalized design may boost productivity and well-being when working remotely.
- Creative work Design: An artist creates a clutter-free, stimulating work area with ideal lighting and plants to promote creativity and attention.
- Collaborative Workspace: A well-designed workplace with soundproofing and adaptable furniture promotes cooperation and communication.

Coping with noise and disruption

Have you ever had to reread a piece several times because someone around was chatting too loudly for you to concentrate? Perhaps you've attempted (and failed) to compose a paper in front of a talkative buddy. If you've ever been in a scenario like this, you know that noise may have a significant impact on performance.

In a 2020 article, Julian Treasure, an international lecturer on sound and communication skills, stated that the most distracting sound is the human voice, although music may also disturb work and productivity. This is especially true in the workplace: if your office is open and full of noisy employees, you are unlikely to get as much work done as if it were quieter.

"Noise and interruptions affect productivity and increase employees' stress, increasing blood pressure and heart rate," stated Dr. Jude Miller Burke, workplace psychologist and author of The Adversity Advantage: Turn Your Childhood

Hardship into Career and Life Success. "It is the rare individual who can day after day, hour after hour, focus well with a constant hum of background noise."

It's simpler to concentrate when you can hear your thoughts over the din of a full organization. But sometimes you don't have a choice: you're imprisoned in a noisy environment and expected to complete your task anyway.

If you work in a noisy environment, there may be a few things you can do to improve it. These eight strategies might help you regain productivity, regardless of the decibel level.

1. Wear earplugs or headphones.

Lynn Taylor, a workplace expert and author of Tame Your Terrible Office Tyrant: How to Manage Childish Boss Behaviour and Thrive in Your Job, stated that earplugs are an excellent choice for individuals who are easily distracted. They reduce background noise and help the brain concentrate.

Taylor also mentioned that you may use your headphones to listen to music. Depending on how sensitive you are to noise, calming music might assist your mind stay focused. Make a playlist that suits you and listen to it when the office becomes unusually loud. You may even feel more motivated or joyful when listening to music.

"Though it may appear strange to add more noise to a loud office, having a small white noise machine app on your phone can help mask any rhythmic sounds with steady, ambient noise," said Stephen Light, CMO and co-owner of Nolah Sleep.

2. Find a quiet room.

Open workstations are sometimes blamed for overhearing regular chats and, in some cases, personal phone calls. While the structure may inspire cooperation, it may also stifle productivity, Taylor explained. If you are unable to focus enough to complete your task, look for a quiet area that is not currently in use to do particularly demanding assignments.

"Find a conference room or empty office that you know isn't off limits [to use] as a haven when you need quiet time," Taylor went on to say.

Additionally, certain times of day may be noisier than others. Plan your tasks based on the volume of the office.

"Keep all your strategic and deep-thinking projects to hours of the day when it's most quiet," Taylor went on to say. "For example, handle more transactional activities when the noise level is higher."

If there is a day when the volume is highest, plan more detailed chores in a different area. Even if you have to share the area with another worker or two, the noise level will be lower than in the full workplace.

3. **Divide up jobs according to your concentration requirements.**

Emails may be sent in a distracting environment, but more intensive tasks, such as writing, reading a lengthy technical paper, or creating a video, require our whole attention, according to Jeff Mains, CEO of Champion Leadership Group.

"Often, these tasks require you to keep a lot of information in your head at the same time to complete them," says Mains. "If you're stopped in the middle of a project, you'll have to go back and retrace your actions to get back on track."

In addition, concentrate on one work at a time and give it your whole attention.

"Oftentimes, employees multitask to accomplish more things faster," said Sonya Schwartz, Her Norm's creator. "However, this will only be achievable if you can concentrate sufficiently in the absence of extraneous noise. Thus, focusing on a single activity will allow you to maintain your productivity.

4. **Expose yourself to loud noises.**

This may appear contradictory, but one of the primary reasons loud noises affect productivity is that we are accustomed to silence.

"Spend more time around constantly noisy environments," stated Brian Nagele, CEO of Restaurant Clicks. "Most individuals will avoid noise to be more productive, but this is not always feasible. Instead, make an intentional effort to position oneself inside the noise."

Nagele stated that this will educate your body to adjust to your surroundings. Those acoustic distractions may eventually fade away from your awareness. Of course, this does not work for everyone, but it is worth a go to reduce the impact of a noisy office on you.

5. Block out your distractions.

A noisy office is enough of a distraction, but you might be exacerbating the effect.

"Try some self-management techniques," said Chris Anderson, the founder of lifestyle portal Soothe Your Feet. "Put your phone aside or set it to quiet mode for now. Close all superfluous browsers and programs, leaving only the one you're currently working on. Make sure you have set periods for breaks and adhere to them as strictly as possible."

Eliminating workplace distractions that you can manage can help you cope with the effects of a noisy office.

Did you know?

According to a Mopria Alliance poll, 55% of office workers are distracted by viewing movies and playing games on their computers or mobile devices.

6. Drown out disturbing noises with other sounds.

Working in a loud workplace might be tough at times since it is difficult to drown out the noise of conversations or music with plainly identifiable lyrics. Experiment with different types of noise.

"Try sitting near an open window to the street where the traffic noise is audible, or sit in a common area with so many people talking that individual conversations become inaudible," said Dean Kaplan, president and chief executive officer of The Kaplan Group

This is akin to utilizing white noise. The distraction may not be the noise itself, but a certain form of noise.

7. Adjust your work schedule.

If you work best when no one else is in the office and it is possible to work outside of typical business hours, consider arriving early or remaining late.

"I once had to come in early to the office before opening hours to complete a deadline that was due at 9 a.m.," said Ally Mashaura, editor-in-chief of Adventures Pursuit. "It was the first time in a long time that I was able to concentrate on my report, which I can only attribute to the fact that there was virtually no one in the office.

Mashaura also stated that most people aren't particularly talkative in the morning, so don't be concerned if you're not the only one arriving at work early.

8. Address the issue.

When everything else fails, be straightforward. Executives, in particular, should stand up and confront individuals who are providing the diversions before things spiral out of control.

"It is up to the leaders in the organization to set the culture for the department, and it is best if the manager can set very clear expectations on unnecessary noise," he added. "Initiate a weekly discourse about noise levels and encourage individuals to address them freely at staff meetings. Set the expectation that if someone is being very loud with personal phone calls, jokes, or daily gossip, you should urge them directly to be quiet."

If you are uncomfortable approaching a coworker, tell a supervisor. Explain that the noise issue is not personal, but you are unable to function to your full capacity as a result. Burke suggests emphasizing that with clear instructions from them, the entire staff might become more productive.

"Maybe it would be worthwhile to discuss the noise level and creative solutions in a staff meeting," she went on to say. "You may be surprised as to the unique solutions that might come up that could be helpful."

Jennifer Post helped write and report on this article. Source interviews were done for an earlier version of this story.

Chapter 10

Overcoming Internal Distractions

In the current world of continual connectedness and information overload, internal distractions—those originating within our minds—pose enormous difficulties to sustained attention, productivity, and general well-being. This chapter discusses effective tactics and approaches for finding, analyzing, and overcoming internal distractions to maximize attentional concentration, boost cognitive function, and foster mental resilience.

The Nature of Internal Distractions

Internal distractions comprise a broad spectrum of mental occurrences that divert attention and disturb cognitive processes:

- Cognitive Biases: Automatic patterns of thought that can lead to incorrect judgments or conclusions, such as confirmation bias (favoring information that supports current ideas) or availability bias (relying on easily available information).
- Emotional Fluctuations: Mood swings, worry, tension, and other emotional states that might interfere with focus and cognitive clarity.
- Habitual Thought Patterns: Repetitive thoughts, mind wandering, and intrusive recollections that take attention away from the work at hand.

Strategies for Managing Internal Distractions

Overcoming internal distractions needs a mix of self-awareness, cognitive control, and emotional management. Here are evidence-based ways for effectively controlling internal distractions:

1. Mindfulness Meditation

Engage in frequent mindfulness meditation activities to improve present-moment awareness and strengthen attentional control. Mindfulness helps notice and detach from distracting ideas, enhancing cognitive clarity and emotional stability.

Example: Dedicate 10-15 minutes each day to mindfulness meditation, concentrating on breath awareness or body scanning to enhance mindfulness abilities.

2. Cognitive Restructuring

Identify and address harmful cognitive biases and negative thinking patterns with cognitive restructuring approaches. Replace erroneous ideas with more realistic and adaptable thought processes to lessen cognitive interference.

Example: When faced with self-doubt before a tough endeavor, question negative beliefs by asking, "What evidence supports this belief? What evidence contradicts it?"

3. Emotional Regulation

Develop emotional regulation abilities to manage stress, anxiety, and other emotional distractions efficiently. Practice relaxation techniques, such as deep breathing or progressive muscle relaxation, to minimize emotional excitation and enhance tranquility.

Example: Use diaphragmatic breathing techniques to soothe the nervous system at periods of heightened stress or emotional intensity.

4. Goal Setting and Prioritization

Set clear, measurable goals and prioritize work to retain attention and reduce distraction. Break down big projects into simple pieces and give specified periods for concentrated effort.

Example: Use the SMART (Specific, Measurable, Achievable, Relevant, Time-bound) framework to develop goals that are clear and achievable.

5. Environmental Optimization

Create a favorable work environment by eliminating external distractions and maximizing workstation ergonomics. A clutter-free, tidy office can increase mental clarity and lessen cognitive burden.

Example: Declutter your office, use noise-canceling headphones to filter out distractions, and create boundaries to limit disruptions during focused work hours.

Real-World Applications of Internal Distraction Management

Apply these tactics to real-world circumstances to illustrate their actual usefulness in reducing internal distractions:

- Professional Setting: An executive employs mindfulness techniques to keep focused during high-pressure meetings and cognitive restructuring to overcome self-doubt.
- Academic Environment: A student uses goal planning and prioritizing to manage study time effectively and decrease procrastination.
- Personal Life: An individual employs emotional regulation skills to cope with anxiety and stress in daily life, boosting overall well-being and resilience

Battling procrastination

Why do so many people postpone and how can you overcome it?

For most individuals procrastination, no of what they claim, is NOT about being lazy. In reality, when we delay we typically work intensively for lengthy stretches immediately before our deadlines. Working long and hard is the reverse of laziness, therefore that can't be the reason we do it. So, why do we procrastinate, and, more importantly, what can we do about it?

As indicated above, some argue they postpone because they are lazy. Others think they "do better" when they postpone and "work best" under pressure. I invite you to be critical and introspective of their explanations. Virtually everyone who claims this frequently procrastinates and has not completed a major academic job in which they formed a strategy, implemented it, had time to evaluate, etc. before their deadline. So, in actuality, they can't draw a comparison concerning the situations they function best under. If you pretty much constantly delay, and never truly approach your job strategically, then you can't honestly assert that you know you "do better" under pressure. Still, other people claim they appreciate the "rush" of leaving things to the last and achieving a deadline. But they frequently say this when they are NOT working under that deadline. They claim this works before or after cramming when they have forgotten the negative repercussions of procrastination such as emotions of anxiety and tension, tiredness, and disappointment from falling below their expectations and having to put their lives on wait for chunks of time. Not to add, leaving things to the last substantially raises the possibility something will go wrong - like falling sick or having a computer problem - and you not be able to pull off the desired grade. So, procrastinating might be terrible for us and raise our chances of failure, yet we do it nonetheless. How come?

Procrastination is not a question, primarily, of having bad time management skills, either, but rather can be connected to deeper and more complicated psychological factors. These dynamics are sometimes made worse by institutions where students are continuously being assessed, especially in college where the pressure for grades is tremendous and a lot might depend on students' success. In actuality, procrastination is typically a self-protection tactic for pupils. For example, if you delay, then you always have the excuse of "not having enough" time if you fail, thus your perception of your abilities is never endangered. When there is so much pressure on achieving a decent score on, for example, a paper, it's no wonder that students want to avoid it and therefore put off their work. For the most part, our motivations for postponing and avoiding are founded in fear and anxiety about performing poorly, doing too well, losing control, seeming dumb, or having one's sense of self or self-concept questioned. We avoid performing labor to prevent our talents from being appraised. And, if we fail to succeed, we feel that much "smarter." So, what can we do to fight our propensity to procrastinate?

Awareness: The First Step

First, to overcome procrastination you need to have an awareness of the REASONS WHY you procrastinate and the purpose procrastination performs in your life. You can't come up with an effective remedy if you don't properly comprehend the basis of the problem. As with other difficulties, awareness and self-knowledge are the keys to figuring out how to quit procrastinating. For a lot of individuals having this understanding about how procrastination prevents them from feeling like they are not able enough, and keeping it in mind when they are tempted to fall into familiar, unproductive, postponing patterns goes a long way to correcting the problem. For instance, two psychologists, Jane Burka, and Lenora Yuen, who have helped many people overcome procrastination, report in their article, "Mind Games Procrastinators Play" (Psychology Today, January 1982), that for many students "understanding the hidden roots of procrastination often seems to weaken them" (p.33). Just recognizing our genuine motives for procrastination makes it simpler to stop.

Time Management Techniques: One Piece of the Puzzle

To combat procrastination time management strategies and tools are necessary, but they are not adequate by themselves. And, not all strategies for managing time are equally beneficial in dealing with procrastination. Certain time management practices are better suited to combating procrastination and others that might make it worse. Those that lessen worry and dread and highlight the joy and rewards of accomplishing tasks function best. Those who are rigid, stressed by the immensity of work, and raise anxiety might induce procrastination and are hence counter-productive. For instance, establishing a long list of "things to do" or arranging every minute of your day may INCREASE your stress and hence procrastination. Instead, make acceptable goals (e.g. a doable list of things to accomplish), break huge activities down, offer yourself flexibility, and assign time to things you like as incentives for a job completed.

Motivation: Finding Productive Reasons for Engaging in Tasks

To combat procrastination it's vital that you stay motivated for PRODUCTIVE REASONS. By productive reasons I mean motives for learning and accomplishing that lead to pleasant, constructive, rewarding feelings and behaviors. These reasons are in contrast to engaging in a task out of fear of failing, not making your parents angry, not looking stupid, or doing better than other people to "show off." While these are all reasons - often very powerful ones - for doing something, they are not productive since they evoke maladaptive, often negative feelings and actions. For example, if you are worried about not seeming foolish you may not ask questions, go into new areas, attempt new approaches, or take the risks necessary to learn new things and reach new heights. A smart strategy to put positive impulses into action is to set and focus on your goals. Identify and write down your motivations for enrolling in a course and evaluate your progress toward your goals using a goal-setting chart. Remember to focus on your reasons and your ambitions. Other people's objectives for you are not goals at all, but duties.

Staying Motivated: Be Active to be Engaged

Another method to avoid procrastination is to keep actively interested in your lessons. If you are inactive in class you're probably not "getting into" the course and its contents, and it undermines your drive. What's more, if you are passive you are probably not making as much sense out of the course and course materials as you might. Nonsense and uncertainty are not engaging; in fact, they are dull and aggravating. We don't typically desire to do tasks that are dull or irritating. Prevent that by aiming to understand course material, not memorize it or just "get through it." Instead, try (1) seeking out what is interesting and relevant to you in the course materials, (2) setting your purpose for every reading and class session, and (3) asking yourself (and others) questions about what you are learning.

Summary of Tips for Overcoming Procrastination

- Awareness - Reflect on the reasons why you procrastinate, your behaviors, and ideas that contribute to procrastination.
- Assess - What feelings contribute to postponing, and how does it make you feel? Are they pleasant, useful feelings: do you wish to alter them?
- Outlook - Alter your perspective. Looking at a major undertaking in terms of smaller bits makes it less frightening. Look for what's intriguing about, or what you want to obtain out of an assignment beyond merely the grade.
- Commit - If you feel stuck, start simply by committing to finish a tiny job, any task, and write it down. Finish it and reward yourself. Write down on your agenda or "to-do" list just what you can truly commit to, and once you write it down, follow through no matter what. By doing so you will progressively develop faith in yourself that you will

truly accomplish what you say you will, something so many procrastinators have lost.
- Surroundings - When performing school work, pick properly where and with whom you are working. Repeatedly placing yourself in circumstances where you don't get anything done - such as "studying" in your bed, at a cafe, or with friends - might be a sort of procrastination, a strategy of avoiding work.
- Goals - Focus on what you want to do, not what you want to avoid. Think about the constructive reasons for accomplishing a job by defining positive, tangible, relevant learning and accomplishment goals for yourself.
- Be Realistic - Achieving objectives and altering habits takes time and work; don't undermine yourself by having high expectations that you cannot accomplish.
- Self-talk — Notice how you are thinking, and talking to yourself. Talk to yourself in ways that remind you of your goals and replace old, counter-productive patterns of self-talk. Instead of saying, "I wish I hadn't... " say, "I will ..."
- Un-schedule — If you feel trapped, you probably won't employ a timetable that is a continuous reminder of everything that you have to accomplish and is all work and no play. So, build a mostly unstructured, flexible timetable in which you fit in just what is required. Keep note of whatever time you spend working toward your objectives and reward yourself for it. This can lessen the emotions

of being overwhelmed and boost pleasure in what you get done.

Swiss Cheese It - Breaking down major jobs into tiny ones is a wise technique. A variation on this is committing short chunks of time to a huge task and completing as much as you can in that period with low expectations about what you will get done. For example, consider spending approximately ten minutes just scribbling down thoughts that occur to mind on the topic of a paper, or skimming through a long book to extract only the important concepts. After doing this numerous times on a major assignment, you will have made some progress on it, you'll have some momentum, you'll have less work to do to complete the task, and it won't appear so massive because you've punched holes in it (like Swiss cheese). In summary, it'll be easier to accomplish the work because you've gotten started and removed some of the impediments to completion.

Handling Mental Blocks

Mental blockages, characterized by a momentary inability to think clearly or do activities efficiently, can greatly restrict growth and productivity in different facets of life. This subchapter discusses practical tactics and approaches for finding, analyzing, and overcoming mental blockages to build creativity, problem-solving abilities, and general mental resilience.

Understanding Mental Blocks

Mental barriers can show in numerous forms and result from diverse psychological factors:

- Creative Blocks: Inhibitions or self-doubt that inhibit creative expression and invention.
- Cognitive Rigidity: Fixed thought patterns or cognitive inflexibility that hinder problem-solving abilities.
- Emotional Barriers: Negative emotions (e.g., fear, worry, frustration) that impair cognitive processes and inhibit decision-making.

Types of Mental Blocks

Identifying typical forms of mental blockages can promote focused intervention and effective resolution:

1. Perceptual Blocks: Difficulty receiving or understanding information effectively owing to prior assumptions or prejudices.
2. Emotional Blocks: Overwhelming emotions (e.g., fear of failure, perfectionism) that limit cognitive functioning and creative inquiry.
3. Cognitive Blocks: Fixed thought habits, mental shortcuts, or cognitive biases that hinder problem-solving skills.

Strategies for Overcoming Mental Blocks

Combatting mental barriers involves a mix of cognitive flexibility, emotional management, and adaptive problem-solving abilities. Here are evidence-based ways to address mental blockages effectively:

1. Identify Underlying Causes

Explore the fundamental reasons for mental obstacles by reflecting on personal beliefs, emotional triggers, or environmental factors leading to cognitive hurdles.

Example: Keep a notebook to document patterns of mental barriers and discover repeating themes or triggers.

2. Practice Mindfulness and Relaxation

Engage in mindfulness meditation and relaxation practices to minimize emotional reactivity and increase mental clarity despite mental barriers.

Example: Incorporate deep breathing techniques or progressive muscle relaxation into everyday activities to reduce stress and boost cognitive resilience.

3. Challenge Limiting Beliefs

Challenge self-limiting ideas and cognitive distortions with cognitive restructuring tools. Replace negative thinking with more balanced and realistic viewpoints.

Example: Reframe "I'll never be good enough" to "I am capable of growth and improvement with effort and persistence."

4. Break Tasks into Manageable Steps

Divide complicated work into smaller, achievable stages to prevent cognitive overwhelm and allow progressive progress.

Example: Break down a huge project into achievable milestones and prioritize work based on urgency and importance.

5. Engage in Divergent Thinking

Cultivate diverse thinking abilities by studying multiple views, brainstorming ideas, and embracing creative experimentation.

Example: Use brainstorming techniques (e.g., mind mapping, free association) to produce novel solutions and overcome creative blockages.

6. Seek Social Support and Feedback

Share issues and seek constructive input from peers, mentors, or trustworthy persons to obtain new ideas and views on overcoming mental blockages.

Example: Collaborate with colleagues or mentors to develop ideas and receive help on addressing cognitive hurdles.

Real-World Applications of Handling Mental Blocks

Apply these tactics to real-world circumstances to illustrate their actual effectiveness in overcoming mental blocks:

- Creative Endeavors: An artist employs mindfulness techniques and divergent thinking to get past creative blockages and explore new artistic possibilities.
- Professional Challenges: A business professional conducts cognitive restructuring and job decomposition to overcome cognitive rigidity and adapt to changing work demands.
- Academic Pursuits: A student utilizes relaxation techniques and seeks peer input to control exam anxiety and increase problem-solving abilities.

Chapter 11

Unleashing Brain Power

Amputees occasionally sense pain, itching, or other impulses from nonexistent limbs while they are experiencing phantom limb symptoms. Tom, a man who had lost one arm, was one of the patients whom neuroscientist Vilayanur S. Ramachandran treated for "phantom limbs."

Ramachandran found that when he caressed Tom's face, Tom sensed that someone was also touching his absent fingers. The somatosensory cortex has distinct regions for each part of the body, and coincidentally, the hand and face regions are next to each other. The neurologist concluded that Tom's somatosensory cortex had undergone an amazing transformation.

Ramachandran concluded that Tom's face-processing cortex had gradually supplanted the hand's domain since the missing hand was no longer providing information to the brain. So his nonexistent fingertips began to feel something when he touched Tom's face.

The adult brain's capacity for self-repair and change is known as neuroplasticity, and this type of rewiring is an illustration of it. Researchers are discovering that the adult brain is significantly more flexible than previously believed. The brain may undergo significant rewiring, or a reorganization of its functions and locations, as a result of our actions and the surroundings. Some people assume that the brain may be reshaped only by our thought patterns.

The creation of new neurons, or neurogenesis, is now understood to be a typical aspect of the adult brain. Studies have revealed that the hippocampus, a structure that is essential for learning and long-term memory, is one of the areas with the highest activity for neurogenesis.

In the olfactory bulb, which is important in processing scents, neurogenesis also occurs. However, not every neuron that is born survives; in fact, the majority of them pass away. The newly formed neurons require connections with existing flourishing neurons as well as nourishment to live. Researchers are now figuring out what influences the pace at which new cells proliferate and how quickly neurogenesis occurs. Exercise, for example, increases neuron survival both physiologically and mentally.

Method 1: Exercise

Wheeled mice have more neurons in their hippocampal regions and exhibit improved learning and memory in tests. Exercise helps enhance the brain's executive functions, which include organizing, multitasking, planning, and more, according to studies on humans. Exercise is also widely recognized for improving mood, and older adults who exercise have a lower risk of developing dementia. Physically active seniors have higher executive function than sedentary ones; even those who have lived life on the sofa might enhance these functions just by beginning to walk more throughout their golden years.

This cognitive enhancement might be caused by several different processes. Exercise improves blood flow to the brain, which helps the brain's hardworking neurons receive more oxygen, fuel, and nutrition. Exercise has been demonstrated to raise levels of a chemical called brain-derived neurotrophic factor (BDNF), which promotes the survival, development, and communication of neurons.

Naturally, none of this research contributes to the understanding of dumb jocks.

In the Front

According to recent studies, adding some music to your workout may even improve it. The volunteers finished two training sessions. They listened to Vivaldi's Four Seasons in one as they perspired to the soothing sound of quiet in the other. Following each exercise, participants answered questions on their verbal and emotional intelligence. Both could be increased with exercise alone, but when exercisers had music to listen to, their verbal scores increased twice as much. Perhaps your insurance provider will cover the cost of a new iPod for you.

Numerous research indicates that exercise also enhances the quality of sleep. as well as immunological function. Does it have any limitations?

Thankfully, you don't have to be Chuck Norris to reap the mental health advantages of exercise. Senior citizen studies have demonstrated that even 20 minutes a day of walking might have a positive effect.

METHOD 2: DIET

Fuel is necessary for both the body and the intellect. What, therefore, will increase your mental capacity, and what will drive you insane? The well-known offender, saturated fat, has no beneficial effects on the brain or body. Humans who consume diets heavy in saturated fat appear to be more susceptible to dementia, and rats on these diets fared worse on tests of learning and memory.

But not all fat is harmful. Since the brain is primarily made of fat (fatty acids are needed for all those cell membranes and myelin coatings), it's critical to consume specific fats, especially omega-3 fats, which are found in nuts, seeds, and seafood. Hypoxic acidemia may be linked to depression, schizophrenia, Alzheimer's disease, and other illnesses.

Superfoods for the brain also seem to include fruits and vegetables. Antioxidants, which fight atoms that might harm brain cells, are abundant in produce. High-antioxidant diets have been shown to prevent brain damage after strokes and even preserve learning and memory in aged rats. That deserves some thinking.

In the Front

Your diet isn't the only thing that impacts your brain. It's also the quantity. Studies have indicated that animals kept in laboratories and fed diets low in calories—anywhere from 25 to 50 percent less than typical—live longer than other animals. They also appear to have greater brain function, as seen by their higher performance on memory and coordination tests. Additionally, mice on low-calorie diets are more resilient to the harm caused by diseases like Alzheimer's, Parkinson's, and Huntington's.

Among the top foods for the brain are spinach, blueberries, and walnuts.

Infants must get adequate fat. Undernourished babies struggle to produce the fatty myelin sheath that supports neuronal signal transmission. Fortunately, 50% of breast milk contains fat for newborns.

>> People who have historically consumed diets rich in omega-3 fatty acids are more likely to be free of central nervous system problems.

METHOD 3: INTRODUCTION

Stimulants are chemicals that stimulate the neurological system, elevating blood pressure, heart rate, energy levels, respiration, and more. Among the group, caffeine is arguably the most well-known. Caffeine increases arousal and alertness by stimulating the central nervous system (it is the most often used "drug" in the world). However, this stimulation may be overdone in excessive levels, leading to nervousness, anxiety, and sleeplessness.

Ramachandran found that when he caressed Tom's face, Tom sensed that someone was also touching his absent fingers. The somatosensory cortex has distinct regions for each part of the body, and coincidentally, the hand and face regions are next to each other. The neurologist concluded that Tom's somatosensory cortex had undergone an amazing transformation.

Ramachandran concluded that Tom's face-processing cortex had gradually supplanted the hand's domain since the missing hand was no longer providing information to the brain. So his nonexistent fingertips began to feel something when he touched Tom's face.

The adult brain's capacity for self-repair and change is known as neuroplasticity, and this type of rewiring is an illustration of it. Researchers are discovering that the adult brain is significantly more flexible than previously believed. The brain may undergo significant rewiring, or a reorganization of its functions and locations, as a result of our actions and the surroundings. Some people assume that the brain may be reshaped only by our thought patterns.

The creation of new neurons, or neurogenesis, is now understood to be a typical aspect of the adult brain. Studies have revealed that the hippocampus, a structure that is essential for learning and long-term memory, is one of the areas with the highest activity for neurogenesis.

In the olfactory bulb, which is important in processing scents, neurogenesis also occurs. However, not every neuron that is born survives; in fact, the majority of them pass away. The newly formed neurons require connections with existing flourishing neurons as well as nourishment to live. Researchers are now figuring out what influences the pace at which new cells proliferate and how quickly neurogenesis occurs. Exercise, for example, increases neuron survival both physiologically and mentally.

According to one study, consuming the same amount of coffee as two cups can improve short-term memory and response time. Additionally, caffeine-fed individuals showed greater activity in attention-related brain areas, according to functional MRI scans performed throughout the research. Furthermore, studies indicate that caffeine may shield older women's memory against age-related loss.

Coffee provides us with about 75% of the caffeine we consume. Aim to consume no more than 100 cups each day. About 10 grams of caffeine, or enough to induce fatal consequences, are present in that amount of coffee.

Among the most well-known stimulant users in fiction is the legendary caper cracker Sherlock Holmes. The investigator frequently talks about how much relief he got from injecting cocaine into his antics. Ensuring that justice is served must be difficult.

METHOD 4: GAME VIDEOS

Your life might be saved by video games. One-third fewer mistakes are made in the operating room by surgeons who play video games for at least a few hours each week than by those who don't. Video games have been found to enhance mental dexterity as well as hand-eye coordination, depth perception, and pattern recognition. Additionally, gamers are more adept at digesting information and maintaining attention spans than the typical person. Nongamers' visual vision improves when they agree to play video games for a week (for scientific purposes, of course). Don't believe that gamers are social misfits either; a study revealed that workers in the white-collar industry who like video games are more self-assured and gregarious.

Naturally, discussing video game impacts would be incomplete without bringing up the widely held belief that video games are to blame for the rise in violent crime in real life. Numerous investigations have confirmed this connection. It appears that young males who play a lot of violent video games have grown desensitized to such portrayals because their brains are less sensitive to visual pictures. Another study found that when players engaged in first-person shooter games, their brain activity patterns were associated with hostility.

It is not a given that these players would behave violently in real life. Though the results do not yet support the theory that the growth in video games is to blame for the rise in juvenile violence, the relationships are still worth investigating.

In the Front

A recent study found that although video games engage the brain's reward pathways, they do so far more in males than in women. Men and women were connected by researchers to operational MRI machines as they engaged in a video game created especially for the study. Although the men's limbic system, which is linked to reward processing, was more active, both groups fared well. Moreover, the males had increased connectivity between the structures that comprise the reward circuit; a player's performance was directly correlated with the quality of this link. In women, there was no such association. When it comes to admitting they feel hooked to video games, males are more than twice as likely as women.

The video game business in the United States is worth $10 billion.

>> In 2003, two police officers and a police dispatcher were shot and murdered by a sixteen-year-old teenager. The family of the victims sued the corporation that created the hugely popular video game Grand Theft Auto two years later. According to the lawsuit, the offender was motivated by his passion for the contentious computer game.

METHOD 5: AUDIO

When Queen's Greatest Hits is played, the auditory cortex examines all of the musical elements, including rhythm, melody, timbre, pitch, and loudness. However, the way that music interacts with the brain is not limited to its inherent sound. In addition to decreasing amygdala activity and stimulating your brain's reward centers, music can help lessen fear and other unpleasant feelings.

A widely reported study revealed that Mozart's listening may improve cognitive function, encouraging parents everywhere to purchase CDs of classical music for their kids. The notion of the "Mozart effect" is still widely held, but the validity of the original study has been called into question, and the benefits of music listening on cognition appear to be modest and transient. Still, there seems to be some positive energy in music. It can help preterm newborns gain weight and be discharged from the hospital earlier. It can also cure anxiety and sleeplessness, decrease blood pressure, and calm individuals suffering from dementia.

Training with music helps strengthen the brain. The brain's two sides are connected via the corpus callosum, cerebellum, and motor cortex, all of which are larger in musicians than in non-musicians. Furthermore, compared to non-players, string players spend a greater portion of their sensory cortex on their fingers. While opinions on whether or not music education increases intelligence are still divided, some research has indicated that early music instruction does help young children's spatial skills.

In the Front

Growing up, learning and performing music enhances the brain stem's receptiveness to spoken sounds. A recent study found that even in children without exceptional musical ability, frequent exposure to music can assist develop the brain stem's extremely basic sound encoding system.

Thus, tone-deaf youngsters everywhere, get up! Chewing on that clarinet is healthy, much like eating veggies.

Cocktail Party Snacks

Singing in your brain might engage the auditory cortex. Just picturing a musical composition triggers the visual brain.

It has been shown that calming and classical music can boost dairy cows' milk production.

METHOD 6: CONSCIENCE

Put apples away. An omelet a day can keep the doctor away if the reams of scientific research supporting this claim are to be accepted (which they generally are). Turning the mind inside for introspection and relaxation—meditation—seems to assist with a wide range of ailments. In addition to anxiety problems, it helps lower pain and treat illnesses including high blood pressure, asthma, insomnia, diabetes, melancholy, and even skin issues. Additionally, consistent meditators report feeling more relaxed and imaginative than non-meditators.

By placing meditators within brain-imaging devices, researchers are now able to shed light on the real alterations in the brain brought about by meditation. For starters, during meditation, brain cells fire in unison, even though they normally activate at various times. Skilled meditators also exhibit spikes in brain activity in the left prefrontal cortex, a region of the brain typically linked to happy feelings. During meditation, individuals with the highest activity in this region also had significant improvements in immune system performance.

The cerebral cortex can thicken as a result of meditation, especially in areas related to sensation and concentration. (The expansion appears to be the consequence of the existing neurons making more connections, the number of support cells increasing, and the enlargement of blood vessels in that location; it does not appear to be the result of the cortex generating new neurons.)

In the Front

Enhancing concentration and focus via meditation can lead to better performance in cognitive activities. Volunteers were taught the Vipassana meditation technique, which focuses on reducing distractions, by researchers over three months. Next, an assignment involving selecting a few numbers from a series of letters was given to the participants. The ability to recognize numbers that momentarily flashed on a computer screen was significantly higher in those who had received meditation instruction. They also appeared to be able to accomplish this with less mental effort.

The monks involved in these scientific investigations have meditated for a minimum of 10,000 hours. That exceeds a year.

The world's biggest meeting of brain experts, the Society for Neuroscience annual conference, included a remarkable speech by the Dalai Lama in 2005.

Chapter 12

Brain configuration and Healing during Addiction Recovery

During addiction recovery, the brain starts a difficult journey to mend and reorganize itself following addiction. This approach may be both intriguing and encouraging for people battling with addiction. Addiction is a chronic condition that has substantial effects on the brain, notably in the ways it may alter critical parts of the brain, such as the prefrontal cortex, which regulates judgment and decision-making. Whether its fentanyl, heroin, or any other substance, substance misuse alters the precise ways neurons interact, adversely altering automatic functioning, memory, emotions, and even perception.

However, there's good news: the brain is highly flexible. Through neuroplasticity, the brain is capable of rewiring and recovering itself after addiction. This brain repair process may sound frightening, but knowing brain healing after addiction can provide compassion for the tenacious route to recovery.

Here we'll study the impacts of chemicals on the brain, including alcohol consumption, and the incredible ability of your brain to recover and rewire itself. Whether you're on the path of recovery or supporting someone who is, knowing the timeframe and science behind these improvements may be tremendously inspiring.

How Long for the Brain to Recovery After Getting Sober?

As you continue on the journey toward recovery, one question that surely sticks in your mind is, how long does it take to rewire the brain after addiction? The answer is hopeful yet complex since the brain begins its mending process quickly after you get clean, but the timeline for full recovery might vary greatly among individuals.

Shortly after reaching sobriety, as early as two weeks after the last use, the beginning symptoms of brain mending may occur. Although there could be sensations of heightened anxiety or sad emotions, these symptoms tend to progressively fade with time and do not suggest a lack of healing. The grey matter of your brain, having shrunk owing to substance addiction, commences its recovery when cell volume returns to normal, which is clear evidence your brain is repairing. In particular, the cerebellum springs into a quick state of rejuvenation shortly after you stop drinking, boosting your coordination and fine motor abilities.

During the detoxification period, typically needed after excessive alcohol usage, favorable brain changes become visible within a couple of weeks. While the restoration of higher cognitive abilities may take a longer extended period to notice, sustained abstinence sets the path for greater tissue volume and general brain function improvements. A broad schedule for brain repair on recovery may look like this:

0-2 weeks: Reduced anxiety and depression symptoms; early grey matter healing occurs and tiny improvements to cognition and function may be observed.

2 months to 5 years: Progressive cognitive restoration, with the range dependent on the individual's specific experience with addiction. Progress is often most noticeable within this time frame, with obvious increases in memory, emotional management, cognition, and reaction.

7 years: Individuals reaching full restoration of brain functioning.

Witnessing constant gains may be immensely comforting. As you sustain a life of sobriety, you'll likely witness greater neuroplasticity, rebalanced neurotransmitters, and emotional stability. Important cognitive traits including long-term memory, focus, and problem-solving skills dramatically increase generally between three to six months post-sobriety, while moods and emotional management continue to stabilize even beyond the one-year mark.

Speed of recovery is impacted by various factors, including the duration and intensity of the preceding addiction to opioids like heroin and fentanyl, and any co-existing diseases. To enhance your brain recovery after addiction, engaging expert help can offer you tools and reinforcement customized to your unique needs for recovery.

Understanding Brain Recovery Post-Addiction

When it comes to the brain healing process after addiction, the main performer is neuroplasticity. Neuroplasticity is your brain's intrinsic capacity to alter, develop, and rearrange itself, and it's the crucial component of brain recovery after addiction. Remarkably, the exact neurocircuits that were formerly impacted by addiction may be altered and reinforced, creating novel paths of behavior and cognition.

Consider these insights about the brain's healing process post-addiction:

Brain healing varies depending on the drug involved: For persons recovering from fentanyl or heroin use, several areas of cognitive function may restart more swiftly due to the shorter lifetime of these substances in the body. In contrast, alcohol addiction, which typically precipitates permanent chemical imbalances and possible neurotoxicity, may need a longer period for the brain to rebalance and heal.

Comprehensive recovery requires a combination of strategies: Regular physical activity and mindfulness activities like meditation contribute greatly to brain repair by increasing neuron development and lowering stress. A balanced diet supports your brain with important nutrients, while consistent sleep patterns stimulate the creation of new, healthy synaptic connections.

Your brain's capacity to heal is nothing short of amazing, and while some damage sustained from alcohol or drug misuse may be irreparable, the possibility for partial or even complete recovery remains

Treatments are available to help in rewiring the brain: Medications such as acamprosate, naltrexone, and disulfiram, intended to block alcohol cravings, can give a foundation for recovery. Concurrently, behavioral healthcare therapies attempt to restore normal function in the brain's reward and stress circuits while strengthening cognitive control.

By accepting a specific treatment plan addressing individual patterns of drug use and related physical, mental, and social difficulties, you may set the way for a durable recovery. It's heartening to know that within months and years of prolonged abstinence, AUD-induced brain alterations may be largely reversed, and other circuits can compensate to restore efficacy in places where function has been damaged. Always remember, that despite the absence of a cure, addiction is curable, and your brain's resiliency serves as a monument to your possibility for recovery.

Key Factors that Influence Recovery Time

The road toward restoring your brain's full capacities post-addiction is a very personal and individual process, impacted by numerous critical elements that can either hasten or delay the duration of recovery other aspects to consider include:

Severity and Duration of Substance Use: Just as deeper scratches take longer to heal, more extended and severe substance addiction often demands a lengthier brain healing period. For instance, if fentanyl or heroin were the chemicals of abuse, the degree of their use might govern how rapidly the brain begins to resume its normal function.

Overall Health and Well-being: Your overall health plays a vital function in brain rehabilitation after addiction. Factors such as a balanced diet, appropriate water, regular exercise, and adequate sleep promote the brain-healing process.

Age and Neuroplasticity: Younger brains tend to exhibit a higher degree of neuroplasticity, which is the brain's capacity to reorganize and adapt. Therefore, age may be a decisive element in the adaptability of your brain recovery following addiction, with younger folks perhaps displaying speedier symptoms of repair.

Psychological Resilience: Factors like stress, worry, and sadness can impair the brain repair process. Developing coping mechanisms and resilience via therapy or self-care routines can assist in an easier recovery path.

Support System: The existence of a robust, positive support network—including friends, family, and addiction recovery groups—can give emotional support and encouragement, playing a critical role in continuing recovery efforts.

Treatment & Rehabilitation Programs: Active involvement in comprehensive treatment programs that address both drug misuse brain damage and any underlying mental health disorders can greatly affect the pace and efficiency of brain recovery after addiction.

By knowing and addressing these essential elements, you may better navigate the route to recovery and appreciate the gains your brain makes each day post-addiction. Embrace the journey with the awareness that each step forward, no matter how tiny, is a monument to the immense resilience and ability for healing that resides inside you and your brain.

The road to brain recovery after addiction is as tough as it is rewarding, thanks to the extraordinary flexibility and resilience of the human brain. We've investigated the essential elements impacting the time it takes to rewire the brain and the complete solutions that help this complicated healing process.

While the timing for recovery may vary, the implications of these observations are clear: with determination and the correct tools, brain rehabilitation is not only achievable but may lead to a rejuvenated sense of self and a satisfying substance-free existence.

Chapter 13

Battling ADHD

Medication is a tool, not a cure for adult ADHD

When you think about treatment for attention deficit hyperactivity disorder (ADHD), previously known as ADD, do you instantly rush to Ritalin or Adderall? Many individuals link ADHD therapy with drugs. But it's crucial to remember that medicine for ADHD doesn't work for everyone, and even when it does help, it won't address all your issues or entirely remove symptoms.

In reality, while medication for ADHD generally improves attention and focus, it often does very little to address symptoms of disorganization, poor time management, forgetfulness, and procrastination—the same characteristics that create the biggest problems for many individuals with ADHD.

Medication for ADHD is more effective when coupled with other therapies. You will get considerably more out of your medicine if you also take advantage of other treatments that address emotional and behavioral disorders and teach you new coping skills.

Everyone responds differently to ADHD medication. Some people report substantial improvement while others get little to no alleviation. The adverse effects also vary from person to person and, for some, they greatly outweigh the advantages. Because everyone responds differently, finding the proper drug and dose takes time.

ADHD medication should always be regularly managed. Medication therapy for ADHD entails more than just taking a medication and forgetting about it. You and your doctor will need to monitor side effects, keep tabs on how you're feeling, and modify the dose accordingly. When medicine for ADHD is not closely controlled, it becomes less effective and more hazardous.

If you want to take medication for ADHD, it doesn't mean you have to stay on it forever. Although it isn't healthy to bounce off and on any medicine repeatedly, you can safely opt to stop treating your ADHD with medication if things aren't going well. If you wish to quit taking medicine, be careful to let your doctor know your plans and work with them to go off your prescription slowly.

Treatment is not restricted to medicine. Any activity you do to control your symptoms might be considered therapy. And while you may want to seek expert aid along the road, ultimately, you are the one in command. You don't have to wait for a diagnosis or rely on doctors. There's a lot you can do to improve yourself—and you can start today.

Regular exercise is a good therapy for ADHD

Exercising frequently is one of the easiest and most effective strategies to minimize the symptoms of ADHD in adults and improve focus, motivation, memory, and mood. Physical exercise burns off surplus energy that might contribute to impulsivity. It also quickly enhances the brain's dopamine, norepinephrine, and serotonin levels—all of which impact concentration and attention. In this approach, exercise and drugs for ADHD such as Ritalin and Adderall operate similarly. But unlike ADHD medication, exercise doesn't require a prescription and it's side-effect-free.

Try to work out on most days. You don't have to go to the gym. A 30-minute stroll four times a week is adequate to bring advantages. Thirty minutes of movement per day is much better.

Pick something pleasurable, so you'll remain with it. Choose activities that appeal to your physical talents or that you find tough yet pleasant. Team sports might be an excellent choice since the social element keeps them engaged.

Get out into nature. Studies demonstrate that spending time in nature helps alleviate the symptoms of ADHD. Double up on the advantages by combining "green time" with exercise. Try hiking, trail running, or strolling in a nearby park or picturesque region.

The relevance of sleep in ADHD treatment

Many individuals with ADHD experience sleep issues. The most prevalent difficulties include:

Trouble trying to sleep at night, generally because racing thoughts are keeping you awake.

Restless sleep. You may toss and turn throughout the night, pull the blankets off, and wake up at each small disturbance.

Difficulty waking up in the morning. Waking up is a daily battle. You may sleep through many alarms and feel drowsy and irritated for hours after getting up.

Poor quality sleep makes the symptoms of ADHD worse, therefore staying on a regular sleep pattern is vital. Improving the quality of your sleep may have a major impact on your attention, focus, and mood.

Tips for obtaining better sleep

Have a predetermined bedtime adhere to it, and wake up at the same time each morning, even if you're weary.

Make sure your bedroom is dark and keep devices out (even the weak light from digital clocks or your cellphone might impair sleep).

Avoid coffee later in the day, or consider cutting it out totally.

Implement a peaceful hour or two before bed. Try to switch off all displays (TV, computer, smartphone, etc.) at least one hour before bedtime.

If your medicine is keeping you awake at night, discuss with your doctor about taking a lesser dose or taking it earlier in the day.

Eating well can help you control ADHD symptoms

When it comes to nutrition, treating ADHD is as much of a question of how you eat as what you consume. Most of the dietary difficulties in people with ADHD are the result of impulsiveness and poor planning. Your objective is to be attentive to your eating habits. That involves planning and buying healthy meals, scheduling meal times, preparing food before you're famished, and keeping healthful, quick snacks on hand so you don't have to dash to the vending machine or grab supper at Burger King.

Schedule frequent meals or snacks no more than three hours apart. Many people with ADHD eat erratically—often going without a meal for hours and then overeating on whatever is nearby. This isn't healthy for your symptoms of ADHD or your mental and physical well-being.

Make sure you're receiving enough zinc, iron, and magnesium in your diet. Consider a daily multivitamin if you're uncertain.

Try to add a little protein and complex carbs to each meal or snack. These meals can help you feel more awake while minimizing hyperactivity. They will also provide you with continuous, enduring energy.

Avoid junk food. While a relationship hasn't been confirmed, many experts feel that food colorings and chemicals typically found in junk foods and drinks may cause or aggravate ADHD symptoms.

Cut back on sweets and caffeine. Many of us consume coffee or eat sugary foods for a temporary energy boost, but that can soon lead to a drop in mood, energy, and attention. Cutting down may help to keep your blood sugar levels constant during the day and enhance your sleep at night.

Add additional omega-3 fatty acids to your diet. A rising number of research demonstrate that omega-3s help mental attention in patients with ADHD. Omega-3s are found in salmon, tuna, sardines, and certain fortified eggs and milk products. While it's more advantageous to receive Omega-3s from food, fish oil, and algae supplements are straightforward methods to improve your consumption.

Choosing a fish oil supplement

The two primary forms of omega-3 fatty acids in fish oil: are EPA and DHA. Supplements differ in the ratio of each. Your best hope for alleviating the symptoms of ADHD is a supplement that includes at least 2-3 times the level of EPA to DHA.

Relaxation strategies to cure adult ADHD

Many of the symptoms of ADHD can be alleviated by relaxing practices such as meditation and yoga. When applied consistently, these calming therapies can boost attention and focus and decrease impulsivity, anxiety, and sadness.

Mindfulness meditation is a technique of concentrated contemplation that soothes the mind and the body and concentrates your thoughts. Researchers suggest that in the long term, meditation boosts activity in the prefrontal cortex, the area of the brain responsible for attention, planning, and impulse control. In a way, meditation is the reverse of ADHD. The purpose of meditation is to teach oneself to focus your attention to obtain insight. So, it's an exercise for your attention span that also could help you comprehend and sort out difficulties. As well as enabling you to better resist distractions, lessen impulsivity, and increase your attention, cultivating mindfulness via meditation may also give you more control over your emotions, something that many adults with ADHD struggle with.

Yoga and similar practices such as tai chi combine the physiological advantages of exercise with the psychological impacts of meditation. It can be especially beneficial if you discover you're too energetic to mediate. You learn deep breathing and other relaxation methods that help you become focused and cognitively aware. By keeping varied positions for lengthy durations, you may build balance and serenity. When you feel overwhelmed or out of control, you may resort to yoga practices to refresh you and bring you back to mental equilibrium.

Therapy for adult ADHD can give you greater coping skills

Treatment for ADHD might sometimes require seeking outside help. Professionals educated in ADHD can help you develop new ways to manage symptoms and modify habits that are causing issues.

Some treatments focus on managing stress and anger or regulating impulsive behaviors, while others teach you how to handle time and money more efficiently and improve your organizational abilities. Many of these methods of therapy are available both in person or through online therapy platforms.

Talk therapy. Adults with ADHD typically suffer from concerns originating from prolonged patterns of underachievement, failure, scholastic difficulty, job turnover, and marital strife. Individual talk therapy may help you cope with this emotional baggage, including poor self-esteem, the emotions of humiliation and shame you may have experienced as a child and adolescent, and resentment at the nagging and criticism you receive from people close to you.

Marriage and family therapy. Marriage and family therapy tackles the issues ADHD can bring in your relationships and family life, such as arguments about money problems, missed obligations, duties in the house, and impulsive actions. Therapy can help you and your loved ones address these concerns and focus on constructive methods of dealing with them and connecting. Therapy can also help your relationships by teaching your partner and family members about ADHD.

Cognitive-behavioral treatment. Cognitive-behavioral therapy teaches you to recognize and alter the negative attitudes and behaviors that are generating issues in your life. Since many persons with ADHD are demoralized by years of effort and missed expectations, one of the major aims of cognitive-behavioral treatment is to convert this negative attitude into a more positive, realistic vision. Cognitive-behavioral treatment also works on the practical challenges that typically occur with ADHD, such as disorganization, work performance problems, and poor time management.

Coaches and professional organizers for adult ADHD

In addition to physicians and therapists, there are several additional experts that may assist you overcome the obstacles of adult ADHD.

Behavioral coaching for adult ADHD is not a typical kind of therapy, but it may be a significant aspect of ADHD treatment. In contrast to traditional therapists who assist people work through emotional difficulties, coaches focus entirely on practical solutions to challenges in everyday life. Behavioral coaches give you skills for arranging your home and work environment, planning your day, prioritizing activities, and managing your money. ADHD coaches may come to your house or chat with you over the phone rather than meet with you in an office; many coach-client interactions are long-distance.

Professional organizers for adult ADHD might be quite beneficial if you have problems arranging your stuff or your time. Organizers can help you decrease clutter, build better organizing methods, and learn to manage your time efficiently. A professional organizer comes to your house or business, looks at how you have things arranged (or not organized), and then offers modifications. In addition to assisting you in managing your papers and bill payments, a professional organizer offers advice for memory and planning tools, file systems, and more. A professional organizer also helps with time management: your tasks, your to-do list, and your calendar.

Conclusion

Congratulations on finishing this trip into the subtleties of attention and distraction control. Throughout this book, we've covered numerous facets of attention, from external distractions like technology interruptions and ambient noise to internal problems such as cognitive biases and emotional fluctuations. We've gone into evidence-based ideas, practical approaches, and real-world applications to help you build concentration and recover your cognitive clarity in today's fast-paced and linked world.

Reflecting on Your Journey

As you approach the finish of this book, take a time to reflect on your journey towards building focus:

- Self-Awareness: Have you obtained insights into your attentional habits and sources of distraction?
- Skill Development: Which tactics and approaches resonated most with you, and how have you implemented them to strengthen your focus?
- problems and Growth: What problems did you experience along the road, and how have you developed in your ability to handle distractions?

Key Takeaways and Insights

Let's outline some major thoughts and ideas from our exploration:

1. External Distractions: Recognize the influence of external stimuli on concentration and adopt environmental improvements to avoid distractions.
2. Internal Distractions: Understand the impact of cognitive biases, emotional swings, and habitual thinking patterns in diverting attention, and utilize mindfulness and cognitive tools to overcome internal obstacles.
3. Deep Work: Embrace the potential of deep work by setting out designated hours for concentrated, undistracted work to increase productivity and creativity.
4. Resilience and Adaptability: Cultivate resilience in the face of distractions by developing adaptable thinking, problem-solving abilities, and emotional management.
5. Balance and Boundaries: Establish appropriate limits with technology, communication, and social contacts to preserve work-life balance and safeguard concentration.

Moving Forward with Purpose

As you go ahead from this book, consider how you will integrate these learnings into your daily life:

- Implementation Plan: Develop a specific action plan for controlling distractions and boosting attention in your profession, school, or leisure hobbies.
- Consistency and Practice: Commit to the constant practice of mindfulness, productivity tools, and boundary-setting procedures to strengthen attention habits.
- Continuous Learning: Stay interested and open to additional investigation of attentional dynamics, productivity strategies, and self-improvement practices.

Embracing the Journey

Remember, building concentration is not a destination but a constant journey of self-discovery and progress. Embrace the process of learning, changing, and perfecting your attention abilities to succeed in an increasingly distracted society.

Final Words of Encouragement

You have the power to reclaim your attention, enhance your productivity, and nurture deep engagement with the present moment. Trust in your abilities to handle distractions with resilience and intention. As you continue on your concentration path, may you find fulfillment, creativity, and meaning in every attempt.

Thank you for beginning this profound journey of attention and distraction control. May the thoughts and strategies provided in this book encourage you to develop sustained attention, uncover your potential, and lead a more focused, meaningful life.

Wishing you clarity, productivity, and success in all your future pursuits!

GOOD LUCK!!!

About the Author

Grant Pierce, Ph.D., is a leading authority in the field of cognitive psychology and personal development. With a deep passion for helping individuals unlock their potential and lead fulfilling lives, Dr. Pierce combines academic expertise with practical insights to empower readers worldwide.

Dr. Pierce holds a Doctorate in Cognitive Psychology from Stanford University, specializing in attentional dynamics and behavior change. His research and experience have culminated in a unique approach to self-help and personal growth, focusing on cultivating focus, resilience, and well-being in a distracted world.

As an accomplished author, Dr. Pierce has authored several best-selling books on productivity, mindfulness, and cognitive enhancement. His work blends scientific rigor with accessible, actionable advice, providing readers with tangible strategies to navigate challenges and thrive in today's fast-paced society.

Dr. Pierce's dedication to empowering individuals extends beyond writing. He is a sought-after speaker, delivering engaging talks and workshops on topics ranging from focus optimization to stress management. His dynamic presentations inspire audiences to take meaningful action towards positive change.

With a commitment to lifelong learning and growth, Dr. Pierce continues to explore cutting-edge research and innovative approaches to personal development. Through his work, he strives to make a lasting impact on individuals seeking to unlock their full potential and lead purposeful, balanced lives.

www.ingramcontent.com/pod-product-compliance
Lightning Source LLC
Chambersburg PA
CBHW052250220526
45471CB00001B/275